MONALISA

Define Yourself

A Step-by-step Guide to Building Your Reputation and the Life of your Dreams

MONALISA

Filament Publishing

Define Yourself is Published by
Filament Publishing Ltd
16, Croydon Road, Waddon, Croydon,
Surrey, CR0 4PA, United Kingdom
Telephone +44 (0)20 8688 2598
Fax +44 (0)20 7183 7186
info@filamentpublishing.com
www.filamentpublishing.com

Author'sWebsite
www.monalisainternational.com

ISBN: 978-1-910125-72-4

Printed by: Berforts Information Press - Stevenage & Hastings

Book Editor: Palden Jenkins

Cover Design: Melissa Love

Layout Design: Lisa Snape

Cover photograph: Armin Weisheit

MONALISA

Define Yourself delivers a simple, straightforward blueprint for anyone who wants to build a powerful, compelling and enduring personal brand. Define and develop, package, distribute and live your personal brand – these are the four strands of the personal branding DNA upon which powerful, compelling and enduring personal brands are built.

I've written this book for anyone who wants to harness the power of a distinctive and compelling personal brand to increase their visibility, credibility and recognition.

MonaLisa

MONALISA

MONALISA

Dedication

For Nefertiti, Light, Life, Love,
Pearl, Juliet and Pamela

-London

"The only person you are destined to become is the person you decide to be."

RALPH WALDO EMERSON
Poet, philosopher and essayist

Contents

"Don't ask yourself what the world needs, ask yourself what makes you come alive, and then go do that. Because what the world needs is people who have come alive."

REV. DR. HOWARD THURMAN
Author, theologian and educator

Your image tells your story.
Be a story worth telling.

MONALISA

FORETHOUGHT

Personal branding is not about achieving status, wealth or fame. It's about taking responsibility for your own happiness and fulfilment. It's about creating a life of value by putting your gifts to their highest use.

STEDMAN GRAHAM

Author, educator and businessman

Successful lives do not just happen. Successful lives are a product of having:

- a clear understanding of *who you are* - your unique qualities, and how you can use these qualities to enhance the value of your life and the lives of those in the world around you;
- a clear vision, purpose and lifelong goals that propel your life forward; and
- an incredible focus, an unstoppable drive and unshakeable resolve to develop your talents into abilities, high performance and enduring success; achieve your life goals and start a revolution.

The absence of the above is a passive approach to life, where you just drift along without significance and no control over where you're going. You expect every direction you take, every outcome you experience, to be down to fate or destiny. The sad truism is that a person who has no control over where he or she is going usually gets nowhere or to the wrong place. As for destiny, destiny is a matter of your daily choices, not chance. Your destiny is not going to come and find you. You have to work for it to achieve it. Life boils down to two simple options: *to act* or *to react.*

- *To act:* To actively create your life by developing your talents into abilities, seeking and finding opportunities that serve your vision and purpose, and building value for yourself and others in the world around you.

- *To react:* To drift along with muddled thinking, taking your talents and abilities for granted, constantly reacting to whatever knocks you may experience, and hoping that something would finally fall into place.

This brings us to the fact that our lives will only go where we direct them. Without direction, we fall into the trap of letting life happen to us, with a resulting overwhelming despair and hopelessness. I've seen many in this pit throw their hands up with the often repeated phrases such as, "*Why me?*" "*I don't know what to do.*" "*I've no choice.*" But, we, you and I know better. There is a choice. There is always a choice. It's this simple: you are in charge of your life and destiny. No matter what you're doing today, you are the writer and director. So my first question to you is:

Are you living purposefully or are you a victim of circumstances?

If you're living purposefully and already committed to creating a life of value, you're well on the way. If you're suffering from the drifting-along malaise and your life is currently a series of accidents, in which you are constantly managing mediocrity and swimming in the shallows of disappointments and stagnation, there is an antidote. The antidote is *personal branding.*

Personal branding will take you from a weak, mediocre existence to a powerful, extraordinary life. It will help you to take control and to envision and create the life you want, by providing you with a system for identifying your value as a human being; planning how you want to function in the world around you; and choosing how you want to be known in that world, in a distinctive, compelling and enduring way. It is a great way for letting others know what you stand for, the value you represent, and for taking responsibility for your actions in all aspects of your life - from your personal life to your work. Also, it provides you with the support system for living the life you've created and for achieving your destiny.

Most successful people define who they are, what makes them unique and their values and aspirations. They build a personal brand based on this, and boldly, thoughtfully and indelibly express themselves through this brand. They use their brand assets to bring value to the world around them.

In this book, we will be creating a personal brand that captures your unique essence, your talents and values, purpose and vision, and your dreams and aspirations. So it should:

- think and see like you;
- look and sound like you; and
- illuminate your grand passion.

At the end of this book, you would have identified your purpose in life, your value as a human being, and how you can nurture and enhance this value through out your lifetime.

Please read each chapter of this book with one thought firmly held in your mind: *we each have just this one life. The thing about time is that it finally runs out. So whether it's thirty years or sixty years you've got left, one day your time will finally run out. All that will remain is the difference you made. So as we move forward and as you plan your greater future, be conscious of time. Use it wisely. Do something positive with yours. Refuse to live a mundane life that is going nowhere. Live a life of purpose. Make a difference. Leave a legacy for those who come after you.*

It's only when we become aware or are reminded that our time is limited that we can channel our energy into truly living...

LUDOVICO EINAUDI

Pianist and composer

No work on building a high quality personal brand will be successful, complete and sustainable without a clear:

- understanding of who you are;
- articulation of your own vision for your life in the choices you make and the actions you take; and
- an investment in the people and the world around you.

You must be confident in your own judgement and maintain a constant and unwavering focus on your vision and image in all your choices and actions. Any choice you make or action you take that is not based on your vision erodes the image you are trying to create. So with every choice you make and with every step you take on this journey, you must keep asking yourself:

- ***What and how is this contributing to my vision and my world?***
- ***How is this contributing to my legacy?***

To paraphrase the physicist, mathematician and writer, Sir Isaac Newton, each of us has breathed better and seen further by standing on the shoulders of giants - by enjoying the legacy left by those who have come before us. We each have a responsibility to give back, to contribute something to our world and to make our lives count. Like the giants before us, we too must get involved in making our world a better place to live. We each have a part to play.

So may we - you and I - embrace *who we are,* live each moment on the edge of possibility, not probability, and commit to:

- becoming our very best self;
- creating outstanding value for others; and
- completing the work we are here to do.

We must be mentally prepared for any challenges that life may throw in our way - no matter what challenges or storms we may face. May I add that storms and challenges are inevitable. No matter how life-altering or catastrophic these storms and challenges are, we must keep working and hoping for the greater future we desire, because *HOPE HAS POWER*. Besides, trials, tribulations and obstacles stretch, mould and make us better than we think we are.

"Let others lead small lives, but not you...
Let others leave their future in someone else's hands, but not you."

JIM ROHN
Entrepreneur, author and motivational speaker

PART I

MONALISA

CHAPTER

1. WHAT IS A PERSONAL BRAND?

Your brand is the truth about you, well told.

OLD ADVERTISING SLOGAN

When you walk into a room, or when people see your name, your online image or profile – how do you think you're perceived? How do they see your brand? If your answer is that you don't have a brand, it's a wrong answer. Whether you've thought of it or not, you already have a personal brand. Every one, home-makers, professional men and women, small business owners, directors of large corporations, mayors of cities, presidents of large nations, leaders of religious groups, nuns ... young, old, man, woman, boy, girl, ... everyone, whatever religion or profession, has a personal brand. Even your dog or cat has a personal brand. And therein lies the key questions to face, which are, if you already have a personal brand:

- ***Are you happy with it?***
- ***Is it compelling and does it work for you?***

Perhaps it may help here to understand what a personal brand is. Because often, the main thing stopping many people from having a compelling personal brand is an array of misconceptions about what a personal brand is or isn't. So, let me begin by dispelling what your personal brand is not. It is not your name, your website, your logo or similar. These are how you tell the story of your brand.

Your personal brand is your reputation. It is what people think, know, feel and say about you, when you're not in front of them. It is the sum of who you are, what you stand for, what you promise, your ability and commitment to keeping this promise and how you add value to your world; the vision, abilities, actions, value system, and so on, that all your possible audiences associate with you.

Your personal brand communicates *who you are, what is unique about you, what you do, what you bring to the table and its benefits* to everyone who shares a part of your life. It defines you, but first, you must define it. Defining, developing and managing your personal brand will help you to understand yourself better, assert your value and meet your highest potential in every aspect of your life, from your personal life to your work. Your personal brand should add value to everything and everyone associated with it.

Every action you take and some actions that you don't take shapes it. Your home decor and location, your appearance, the way you enter a room, your body language, your handshake, the way you communicate and interact with others, your website, your online profiles and conversations, your blog posts, your tweets, your business documents, and more, all add up to define your personal brand - *how people see you*. So your personal brand is the sum of every small gesture, every single thing you do - good, bad, beautiful, ugly - held in the minds of others. You do not have complete control over it, but you can conduct and influence it by what you do today and tomorrow.

So, let me finish this chapter by asking you the following:

- ***What is your personal brand currently saying about you?***
  - ***Is it clear and positive?***
  - ***What does it promise?***
  - ***What value does it represent?***
  - ***Is it working effectively for your vision?***
- ***Is it the distinctive, compelling and enduring brand you need for your greater future?***
- ***Do you need to develop or expand it?***

Your personal brand is the powerful, clear, positive idea that comes to mind whenever other people think of you. It is what you stand for; the values, abilities and actions others associate with you.

DARREN HARDY
Author and publisher

CHAPTER

2. HOW A PERSONAL BRAND CAN BENEFIT YOU

Regardless of age, regardless of position, regardless of the business we happen to be in, all of us need to understand the importance of branding. We are CEOs of our own companies: Me Inc. To be in business today, your most important job is to be head marketer for the brand called You.

TOM PETERS

Business author and speaker

I said earlier that everyone has a personal brand, and that your personal brand is what people think, know, feel and say about you, when you're not in front of them. You may be wondering how much you should care or whether you should care at all about what people think, feel or say. How much should you really focus on *Me Inc*?

There are two schools of thought on *personal branding*. The first school of thought believes that being so concerned about what others think about us is insincere and that the more emphasis we place on *Me Inc*, the less we are really able to focus on the key issues in our environment or our jobs. They argue that personal branding can only take a poor secondary consideration in a highly competitive, incredibly difficult and unstable economy, in which the daily grind of surviving is challenging enough and has stripped many of the time and pleasure of creating and managing their reputation.

The second school of thought argues that we should care about what people think about us, because it has a direct influence on how they react toward us and that this can either expand or limit what we are going to accomplish in our lives. They say that personal branding cannot be perceived as insincere because its main goal is to project the true image of a person. This school of thought suggests that instead of struggling to survive in a difficult and unstable economy, where many people are underpaid and undervalued for their work and contribution, we should work diligently at building a powerful personal brand that will assert and leverage our value, helping us achieve our life's vision, purpose and goals.

They argue that survival in a difficult economy requires more action, not less. When the economy is difficult, the strong and bold overtake or crush the vulnerable, because they are able to pull out all the stops to differentiate themselves. This school believes that a high quality brand that yields a valuable output will thrive in any economy. A distinctive, engaging and compelling personal brand is often the difference between:

- great success and mediocrity;
- being merely competent at what you do and consistent great performance;
- merely surviving as one of the pack and succeeding as a top-tier professional or entrepreneur or creative contributor.

My observation is that to succeed, thrive and be sustainable in both your personal and business life, in today's diverse, fiercely competitive and multi-threat environment, talent, ability and hard work are no longer enough. People are too busy to figure out what your goals or accomplishments are, your unique skills set and what you bring to the table. It is so easy to get lost in the sea of other talented, hardworking and perfectly capable people. But thankfully, because no two people are the same, having control of your personal brand means that you can thoughtfully highlight, leverage and celebrate what makes you different and unique - *your personal experience, insights and your skills set.*

Of course, you can just focus on your work and your life and hope that by sheer luck or some divine intervention, your accomplishments will be discovered like precious gold in a mine and that your talents, abilities and the value your provide will be noticed in the sea of other talents and adequately rewarded. Or, you can strategically let others know what you are good at, the value you provide, your accomplishments and your points of distinction and power. Personal branding provides you with the framework to do the latter.

If you believe in the philosophy of the second school of thought, which says that the image you project influences what others think of you and how they react to you, then personal branding is for you. It will help you to:

- share your vision with others and inspire them to want to share a part of their lives with you;
- pull away from the crowd and leverage your points of distinction and power;
- take giant steps towards the achievement of your personal and business goals, by developing your talents into abilities and demonstrating excellence or sufficient expertise in your work - *your power lies in the fundamentals of your expertise*; and
- have control over what you project to others by providing yourself with a framework for living an authentic and holistic life.

"You have to understand your own personal DNA. Don't do things because I do them or Steve Jobs or Mark Cuban tried it. You need to know your personal brand and stay true to it."

GARY VAYNERCHUK
Author and public speaker

I believe that wherever your life is at the moment, it will become more meaningful, powerful and valuable, when it is guided by your personal brand. But first, let's look at what developing your personal brand will deliver to you. Understanding some of the benefits of a personal brand will help you decide whether you want to create one.

2.1. PERCEPTION MANAGEMENT

Accept no one's definition of your life, define yourself.

HARVEY FIERSTEIN

Actor and playwright

Personal branding is about managing your name and others' perception of you. We now live in a digital world of misinformation, Google records and social networks. People form perceptions and opinions of you based on the information they get from a simple search online and from word of mouth on you. The first step for a future client, recruiter, boyfriend or girlfriend, to find out a little more about you or to verify that you are who you say you are, is to Google you. They search to see what people are saying about you, what projects and activities you've done or are actively involved in.

They start forming an opinion about you from the first page of any such search. As you well know, a search will only generate information it finds. If unflattering information is all that is available on you, that's what people will see. When it comes to work or relationships, people often decide whether they want to know you better, based on your reputation.

"When you brand yourself properly, the competition becomes irrelevant."

DAN SCHAWBEL
Millennial Branding

Whether you're meeting a client for the first time or going on a first date, it really helps if they've heard and read good content about you. Personal branding emboldens you to magnify your great qualities and to drive down what you don't want people to read about you with more positive content. Defining, developing and managing your personal brand means that you drive the conversation about who you are, your abilities and the outcomes others can expect from you.

Distributing and managing your personal brand on highly optimised sites or social networks will magnify the most relevant information about you, ensuring that the attributes, key message and unique promise of your brand appear high up on the search engine page. This gives you some credibility to build on at any meeting. Failure to define your brand means that others will define it for you, by drawing conclusions based on a shallow set of visual encounters, filtered through their prejudices. The stronger you make your brand, the more control you have over others' perception of you, especially in the business world where perception is everything.

EXERCISE 1

Google yourself to see what information is out there about you. Don't stop on the first page.

- Make sure there is no false information about you online. If there is, you should ask the people responsible for publishing the information to remove it. You may need to involve your lawyer, if they refuse, but this is highly unlikely. Alternatively, feed in information that counteracts or counterbalances it.

2.2. VISIBILITY AND INSTANT RECOGNITION IN OUR OVERCROWDED MARKETPLACE

The rules for growth and success have changed considerably in the past few years. It is no longer enough to rely on education and climbing-up some corporate ladder for your future. In fact, there is no more ladder. Globalisation, helped along by the recent communication revolution; the internet and the proliferation of online social media has flattened our world and created epic levels of competition. In the new hyper-connected digital age, over three billion of us are connected to each other on the internet. Our ability to share information at lightning speed and from any part of the world means that most of us are now able to operate in a global market. With everyone now coming online and joining the conversation, there is information overload.

It can be a daunting task to get yourself heard by your target audience, let alone gain recognition for what you do well. These days, those who most succeed are those who stand out from the crowd by building lasting value in everything they do. Personal branding breaks through the noise by giving you a distinctive identity and separating you from the pack. It requires you to define, develop and communicate what makes you unique - your unique talents, abilities and the value you add to others' lives.

A high quality personal brand makes the value you provide tangible, giving you visibility and a compelling identity that is easily and instantly recognised when encountered by others. This will attract people who want the unique promise of your brand and could open doors to further opportunities that are beyond your vision - collaborations with your peers, partnerships, joint ventures, trade and financial connections, and so on.

2.3. GREATER JOB SATISFACTION AND INCOME

As an individual, you're a CEO of one, and you have a duty to maximise your profits.

CAMERON KENG
Tax, finance and business expert

Because of the recent recession and the fear created around it in the media, many businesses and organisations decreased or froze the salaries of their employees. Whilst this strategy to reduce costs or to maximise their profits is understandable and accepted by their employees, desperate to hold on to their jobs during the recession, the concern now is that the salary expectation for many employees have remained unchanged. A strategy that was expected to be short term seems to have been adopted for the longer term by many companies.

However, according to an article by Cameron Keng, a tax, finance and business expert in Forbes Magazine, June 2014, there is a global shortage of human capital and skilled workers. Companies around the world are competing for talent and are willing to negotiate better conditions and greater pay when hiring, if it means they can hire the expert. Personal branding provides you with a framework to demonstrate and leverage excellence or expertise to attract greater opportunities or, as in this case, greater job satisfaction and pay. Having a high quality personal brand that yields a valuable output can make a huge difference in the opportunities that you are presented with as well as your income and career path.

"This above all: to thine own self be true,
And it must follow, as the night the day,
Thou canst not then be false to any man."

WILLIAM SHAKESPEARE
Hamlet, Act 1, Scene 3

2.4. GREATER SELF KNOWLEDGE AND AUTHENTICITY

Your personal brand enhances your self knowledge and gives you authenticity. The process of developing, maintaining and in some cases extending your personal brand requires you to develop an immense understanding of *who you are* and to commit to optimising your talents and abilities. It is concerned primarily with how to create the best authentic '*you*' and how to project your true image. It keeps you at the forefront of what is important to you and your target audience. It also helps you to maintain a balance between your personal and business objectives. If you:

- are clear about *who you are* and your points of difference;
- remain true to your values, abilities and purpose; and
- focus on what is important to you and your target audience;

you will not only be authentic, but people will trust and believe in you because you can make a connection with their lives, needs and aspirations. Great personal brands endure because people learn that they are stable and credible, and trust them to be what they say they are. *Who they are* and *what they say* are integrated with *what they do*.

"Life isn't about finding yourself. Life is about creating yourself."

GEORGE BERNARD SHAW

Dramatist and co-founder of the London School of Economics

2.5. LIFE PLANNING

Your brand helps you with life planning. Personal branding requires you to be crystal clear about what you want to achieve in life and the difference you want to make in others' lives, and it helps you set goals to get there. It provides you with a system for defining your purpose and life goals, and forces you to pinpoint with utmost clarity, what you are good at and known for, and how you can use your talents and abilities to achieve your life goals more effectively and quickly.

2.6. COMPETITIVE AND VALUABLE IN OUR CONSTANTLY CHANGING ENVIRONMENT

The world has changed greatly in the past few years and continues to change. Our lives are now a maze, with moves sideways, forwards and backwards. It is likely that your career or relationships will take you to several places in the next few years. The only thing that will remain constant and keep you competitive and valuable, no matter what the future brings, is your personal brand.

Personal branding offers resilience and security. No matter how the economy or your life evolves, the brand that is you will remain fundamentally the same, because it stands for something unique. It stands for your vision and purpose, which does not significantly change over your lifetime. Of course your purpose could expand as you grow, but its main focus hardly ever changes. Your personal brand is your greatest asset for asserting your value in both your business and personal relationships and, if maintained, it will continue to add value to everything and everyone associated with it.

"Go confidently in the direction of your dreams. Live the life you've imagined."

HENRY DAVID THOREAU
Author, poet and philosopher

2.7. GREATER INFLUENCE

Personal branding is clearly communicating the unique promise of value that you offer.

WILLIAM ARRUDA

Founder, Reach Branding Club

Your brand is an asset that will help you to expand your influence. If you:

- build it well,
- communicate clearly what makes it relevant to your target audience, and
- deliver consistently on its unique promise,

your personal brand will then dramatically increase your credibility and influence, enabling you to make a bigger difference. It will also bring you friends, clients and revenue, even when you are not working. Your personal brand creates wealth for you when others are enthusiastic about you, because you've made a real contribution. It is not what you say about your brand that makes it valuable and influential, it is what others say about you, which is far more powerful.

"Try not to become a man of success, but rather a man of value."

ALBERT EINSTEIN
Theoretical physicist

SOME STRONG PERSONAL BRANDS	
Photography	Mario Testino, Annie Leibovitz, David Bailey
Fashion	Vivienne Westwood, Ralph Lauren, Tom Ford
Music	Madonna, Lady Gaga, Elton John
Filmmaking	Steven Spielberg, Martin Scorsese, Quentin Tarantino
Acting	George Clooney, Meryl Streep, Angelina Jolie
Politics	Barack Obama, Angela Merkel, Aung San Suu Kyi
Business	Sir Richard Branson, Sir Alan Sugar, Bill Gates
Cooking	Nigella Lawson, Heston Blumenthal, Gordon Ramsay
Sports	David Beckham, Andy Murray, Venus Williams

Would you agree that each of these powerful personal brands is very visible, influential and an asset?

Apart from the fact that their brands earn them a significant income from product endorsements, public appearances, licensing deals, book deals, speaking fees and more, each of them have transcended the boundaries of their categories to become a brand of iconic stature, surrounded by a real buzz, perceived by their audience to deliver real value.

Nothing can hold you back,
except the doubt in your eyes.

MONALISA

CHAPTER

3. BREAKING UP WITH MEDIOCRITY

Personal branding is about standing for something in a big way and asserting yourself honestly and boldly. It's about casting aside the limitations and pressures imposed by what you've been told that you can or cannot be or do and expanding your vision, going for the very best and becoming your very best. If you want to present the best possible you, to play your biggest game possible, to live your best life, you will need to reach beyond any self or other imposed barriers and limitations for your biggest possibility. To create a distinctive, compelling and enduring personal brand that will attract and engage all your possible audiences, you need to be rid of any inhibitors or blocks that undermine your self-image and stop you from honest and bold self-expression. You cannot allow any obstacle - fears, self-doubts, limiting beliefs, a victim mentality, restrictive habits or culture - to hold you back. It is only when you've banished all obstacles from your life, that you can fully concentrate on creating the life you desire. In creating your personal brand, you cannot present a weaker version of yourself. A weaker version of you will restrict you to mediocrity. Only bold, honest and positive self-expression can catapult you into the greater life you aspire to.

There is no passion to be found playing small - in settling for a life that is less than the one you are capable of living.

NELSON MANDELA

President of South Africa, 1994-99

"It is remarkable how much mediocrity we live with, surrounding ourselves with daily reminders that the average is acceptable. Our world suffers from terminal normality. Take a moment to assess all the things around you that promote your being 'average.' These are the things that keep you powerless to go beyond a 'limit' you arbitrarily set for yourself."

STEWART EMERY
Professor and author

The most difficult place to make a sustainable change is often in your personal presentation. This is because the biggest obstacle you face here is yourself. Your intention may be to present yourself as a confident, wildly successful consultant or coach or entrepreneur or artist, but you may also have other, less conscious intentions, which include gaining the love and approval of members of the different groups you belong to or, worse, negative beliefs in your head that stop you from putting your truth out there in front of others. So depending on whose company you are in – your peers, business friends, fellow club members or your family members, and on how confident you are feeling at any given time, you make up huge stories in your head about what is expected of you, about what you can or cannot be or do and then take on a completely different persona from what you intended, to meet these self-imposed expectations and limitations.

As the philosopher, educator and author Eric Hoffer once said, ***"No matter what our achievements might be, we think well of ourselves only in rare moments. We need people to bear witness against our inner judge, who keeps book on our shortcomings and transgressions. We need people to convince us that we are not as bad as we think we are"***. Many times, when we don't act as we should, it is often because we don't believe in ourselves. Some research that began in 1978 by the psychotherapists, Dr. Pauline Rose Clance and Dr. Suzanne Imes found that many high achievers, mostly women, suffer from Impostor Syndrome, a personality trait which leaves them in constant self-doubt and unable to acknowledge their attractiveness, competences or accomplishments. Even though the term Impostor Syndrome was coined by Dr. Clance and Dr. Imes in their 1978 research, further studies in the last three decades on this psychological phenomenon found that the

Impostor Syndrome has plagued many high-performing men and women for decades. Even Albert Einstein suffered from the *Impostor Syndrome* towards the end of his life.

The exaggerated esteem in which my lifework is held makes me very ill at ease. I feel compelled to think of myself as an involuntary swindler.

ALBERT EINSTEIN TO QUEEN ELISABETH OF BELGIUM, MARCH 1955

From *Time Bandits*, Jim Holt

Irrespective of their achievements, those who suffer from this syndrome tend to hold on to their childhood dramas, insecurities and traumas. They attribute their successes to external factors and struggle to accept their own worth. They feel that they are not smart, talented or experienced enough for their achievements or aspirations. They constantly feel that they are a fraud and fear that they would soon be found out. They don't think big.

In fact, generally, not many of us really think big enough. According to the psychiatrist, Carl Gustav Jung, "***We walk around in shoes far too small for us".*** This becomes a real concern when we allow our self-doubt, limited thinking and fear to stop us from asserting ourselves and from taking the necessary actions to achieve our higher aspirations. If this is you, an objective analysis of your achievements will confirm to you that the condemning voice in your head is contrary to your reality. You are attractive, wonderful and have significant value. If truth be told, your achievements so far did not happen by accident. You did play a significant role.

Whatever you think you are worth at this moment, multiply it by a hundred and you would only have begun to understand your true value. You don't have to be the best to create outstanding value. To be extraordinary, you need to focus on the unique value you bring to your world - on the unique way that you enrich the lives of others. Don't compare your insecurities and challenges with the outer projections of excellence you believe others have - they may in turn be comparing their own insecurities and challenges to your own projections of excellence. The truth is that anyone who is growing and making a difference is struggling and stretching too. It's not as effortless as it may seem. Nothing worthwhile is really ever achieved without a struggle.

It's not what you are that holds you back, it's what you think you're not.

DENIS WAITLEY

Author and motivational speaker

What we believe others expect of us or what we think we see in others, is often what is in us. When we make a decision about our future, the only opinion that matters is what we think of ourselves and our decision. How others choose to respond to our decision is more to do with them than us. It shouldn't therefore affect our behaviour at all. At the end of the day, the only thing that counts is how we feel and what we think of ourselves. What we think matters so much because it affects our behaviour, and our behaviour controls our future. So get past your self-doubt and stop the negative and crazy chatter in your head that tells you that you are not good enough. This way, you can face into your challenges and aspirations, embracing your potential and achieving your destiny.

Any time you take on a persona to please someone else, you take away your freedom to be truly you. We are programmed to want to be liked. Know that any time you try to adapt yourself to what you think will please others, you weaken your personal brand. The result is that you end up with a weak and confusing brand identity. The important truth is that your brand cannot and should not appeal to everyone.

To be loved and approved of by everyone, you would have to become so indistinct and changeable that *who you are* becomes almost meaningless. If people doubt your authenticity, they will withdraw from you anyway. We are extraordinary when we share who we truly are. We are extraordinary when we are authentic. So, don't ever give up your right to be your best authentic self. Always exercise your free will to be *who you are*. You honour yourself when you vigorously advocate what you believe, align your actions with *who you ar*e and go after what you want. I implore you to own your successes and what you want for your future. You will not achieve your dreams until you start believing in yourself, until you start believing in *who you are*. Give your self permission to be who you want to be. Seek the change you want. Don't seek approval.

Every time you suppress some part of yourself or allow others to play you small, you are in essence ignoring the owner's manual your creator gave you and destroying your design.

OPRAH WINFREY

Television mogul and actress

Also, sometimes, as we begin to make personal changes in our lives, some of our loved ones may feel threatened by the process of change. We might be married to one of them or the daughter or son or sister or brother of one of them. Whilst they genuinely want us to be successful, they may be highly invested in one or two things: first, in their own wish for us to do what fits their vision of us; and second, in maintaining their own comfort zone by keeping us in ours. So if they tell you that you can't, know that it is more to do with their own limits than yours. Don't allow their limits to compromise *who you are*. Anytime you hear someone say that you can't, get away from them quickly. You mustn't allow any negativity to slip into your subconscious. If you hear that voice inside you doubting yourself because of what you've heard, stand up and say out loudly, 'Yes, I can,' and move firmly into the world of 'Yes, I can and will.'

However, in the main, those who truly care about you would love you to become your very best authentic self. Where this is not the case, you must remain firm in your resolve. It may help to share your concerns with all those involved and explain clearly why the changes you are making are important to you. If this doesn't help, you will need to step past any criticism, cynicism or other negative attitude to become who you must be, even if that means going it alone for a while. Ultimately, it is your responsibility to make sure that you surround yourself only with people who believe in you, people who lift you up and make you stronger.

Please also note that anytime we make a change in our lives, we are often required to give something up. This is usually something that is holding us back from growth. And though it may seem like a great loss at the time, we will come to see that whatever we give up during this time needed to go.

Finally, another common self-imposed barrier to bold self-expression is perfectionism. Please let us not confuse perfectionism with attention to detail, which is extremely important in personal branding. Of course the details matter, but when your focus on certain details stands in your way of making important decisions, they become a barrier.

"You're going to find naysayers in every turn that you make. Don't listen. Just visualise your goal, know exactly where you want to go. Trust yourself. Get out there and work like hell. Break some of the rules and never ever be afraid of failure."

ARNOLD SCHWARZENEGGER
Actor, filmmaker and politician

Perfectionism can be a way of avoiding failure or of procrastinating instead of facing a challenging task. For example, you may say that you're waiting to loose a few kilos first or to get rid of some spots on your face, before commissioning a portrait shoot for your website and personal publicity campaign. But, what is really the main reason for not commissioning your portrait shoot? Losing a few kilos first or improving your skin is a great idea, but you've got to ask yourself whether this is a fixed target that you are committed to achieving, with an effective diet and exercise plan or skin health and care routine, or whether this is just an excuse to postpone moving ahead with essential work to develop your personal brand. If your wish hasn't got actions behind it, it is simply a fantasy and an excuse, and you must immediately eliminate it from your path to growth. We all know that the time for growth will never be absolutely right, so don't set it aside until another day. For those who really desire it, growth starts with a decision. One step at a time, with each step improving the landscape under which you are growing.

Put blinders on to those things that conspire to hold you back, especially the ones in your own head.

MERYL STREEP

Actress

EXERCISE 2

Before we start crafting your personal brand, I would like you to consider each of the following questions. Please don't just think your answers, write them down. Writing down your answers disciplines you to be more honest with your response.

- What do you hate? I mean, *what do you really hate*? - Do you hate rejection, failure, mediocrity, small thinking, not being appreciated, not being respected, a victim mentality, injustice, war, bad governance, political instability, ignorance, poverty, cancer, environmental pollution, unequal educational systems, racism, violence, mistreatment of women, child abuse, corporate slavery...?

    - Why do you hate it?

    - How does it make you feel? - Does it make you angry? Does it make you want to cry?

- What or who is your enemy?

You have enemies? Good. That means you've stood up for something, sometime in your life.

WINSTON CHURCHILL
Former Prime Minister of the United Kingdom

Yes, we all have an enemy. Naming and facing your enemy is important. Why? Because it will help your growth and success and it may even eliminate that enemy. James Arthur Baldwin, the American novelist, essayist and playwright said that, ***"Not everything that is faced can be changed, but nothing can be changed until it is faced"***.

You have to confront what or who frightens you; what holds you back from growth. You cannot afford to play the ostrich and bury your head in the sand, hoping that they will miraculously disappear, and there is no magic wand that you can wave to get rid of your enemies. You have to face them down. If you don't, their hold on you will get stronger and stronger. So you really have no choice but to fight. My observation is that it is far more powerful and fruitful to become a person with a cause than a person with a grievance. When you are face to face with an enemy, you are up against a discovery about your true strength, because until you've faced and fought your enemy with everything you've got, you'll never discover how strong you are.

What frightens me most is how quickly many people settle to what they call *their lot*. A bullying boss or partner who frequently undermines your existence, or racism or corporate slavery ... whatever yours may be, you've got to face and fight it. You've got to fight it with everything you've got, even if you think you'd lose and especially when some conventional thinking recommends that it may be easier to roll over. We've all heard the crowded conversation,

> ***"He's deluded. Surely, he knows he'll fail. You don't fight an enemy with much bigger resources, with a superior education, an army of supporters... You'll not win. You'd be crushed!"***

Wrong! My observation is that several other factors play into winning. The most important factors are what's inside your head and your level of courage and self-belief. But before courage, self-belief and their equally important relatives, there's one critical step that you must first take. You must get mad. You must get crazy. Because nothing happens until you get really, really crazy. This is the main thing that will give you a chance of winning - a chance to make the world a better place. This is only possible when you join the band of crazies, misfits and rebels, who made our world a better place to live, through their radical choices and actions. So,

Here's to the crazy ones, the misfits, the rebels, the troublemakers, the round pegs in the square holes, the ones who see things differently – they're not fond of rules, and they have no respect for the status quo. You can quote them, disagree with them, glorify or vilify them, but the only thing you can't do is ignore them because they change things. They push the human race forward, and while some may see them as the crazy ones, we see genius, because the people who are crazy enough to think that they can change the world, are the ones who do.

STEVE JOBS
Entrepreneur, inventor and co-founder of Apple

I don't have enough space in this book to recount many of the stories of all the crazy ones who faced their enemies, who withstood some discomfort for their fight, and whose fight started a domino effect that did not just change their circumstances but changed our world for the better. The portraits of these extraordinary, visionary human beings and their extraordinary journeys have kept me awake many nights. Their stories have taught me about courage, sacrifice and individual dignity, inspiring me to be the change I desire. I am greatly inspired, challenged and encouraged by:

- *William Wilberforce*, who tirelessly fought for the *abolition of the slave trade* and subsequently of slavery itself. Wilberforce faced fierce opposition from those making fortunes from the slave trade, including the church. He headed the campaign against the trade until the passage of the Slave Trade Act of 1807, and the campaign for the abolition of slavery, which led to the Slavery Abolition Act of 1933.

If to be feelingly alive to the sufferings of my fellow creatures is to be a fanatic, I am one of the most incurable fanatics ever permitted to be at large.

WILLIAM WILBERFORCE

Politician and social reformer

- Irena Sendler, the Polish social worker and activist, who served in the Polish Underground as head of the Żegota children's section in German-occupied Warsaw. Irena Sendler, with the help of about 24 other Żegota members, risked her life to smuggle some 2,500 Jewish children out of the Warsaw ghetto, saving these children during the Holocaust. She was arrested and tortured by the Gestapo and sentenced to death for her actions, but she was saved on the way to her execution. Irena survived the war and was awarded Poland's highest honour - the Order of the White Eagle - and she appears on a 2009 Polish commemorative coin.

Every child saved with my help is the justification of my existence on this Earth, and not a title to glory.

IRENA SENDLER

Letter to the Polish Senate in 2007

- *Martin Luther King, Jr.*, who fought *racial inequality* and *poverty*. During his fight, *Martin Luther King* delivered one of the most significant speeches in history. His ***'I have a dream'*** *speech,* about his vision for the future of blacks in America, delivered on the steps of the Lincoln Memorial on 28 August, 1963, inspired the world and remains the cornerstone of the self-image of many successful blacks in the world.

You may be 38 years old, as I happen to be. And one day, some great opportunity stands before you and calls you to stand up for some great principle, some great issue, some great cause. And you refuse to do it because you are afraid ... You refuse to do it because you want to live longer ... You're afraid that you will lose your job, or you are afraid that you will be criticised or that you will lose your popularity, or you're afraid that somebody will stab you, or shoot at you or bomb your house; so you refuse to take the stand. Well, you may go on and live until you are 90, but you're just as dead at 38 as you would be at 90. And the cessation of breathing in your life is but the belated announcement of an earlier death of the spirit.

DR. MARTIN LUTHER KING, JR.
Clergyman, activist and leader

- *Rosa Parks,* who fought *racial inequality.* Rosa refused to give up her seat on a bus for a white man on 1 December, 1955, and was arrested for civil disobedience and fined. This sparked the 13-month Montgomery Bus Boycott, which led to the

1956 Supreme Court decision banning segregation on public transportation. Rosa fought against racial injustice and for civil rights and became known as a symbol of courage.

I have learned over the years that when one's mind is made up, this diminishes fear; knowing what must be done does away with fear.

ROSA PARKS

Civil rights activist

- *Nelson Mandela,* who fought *apartheid.* Nelson Mandela fought for the freedom of his fellow blacks in South Africa. Against overwhelming odds, he uncompromisingly achieved his dream of equality for all South Africans after serving twenty-seven years in prison, and became a champion of individual dignity and freedom and for peace and reconciliation. Mandela went from prisoner to president and proved that even imprisonment cannot stop us, when we are fighting for a cause much bigger than us.

I have fought against white domination, and I have fought against black domination. I have cherished the ideal of a democratic and free society in which all persons live together in harmony and with equal opportunities. It is an ideal which I hope to live for and to achieve. But if needs be, it is an ideal for which I am prepared to die.

NELSON MANDELA

'Speech from the Dock', 20 April, 1964

- *Mother Teresa,* who fought *poverty,* devoting her life to caring for the sick and poor. Mother Teresa founded the Order of the Missionaries of Charity, a congregation of Roman Catholic women dedicated to helping the sick and poor. She became a symbol of peace and international understanding, receiving the Nobel Peace Prize for her humanitarian work.

A life not lived for others is not a life.

MOTHER TERESA
Nun and missionary

My list goes on and on and on. There are millions of men and women in our time, who have faced a bigger enemy, risking their lives on the possibility that they could make the world a better place for all. They did not wish or wait for the world to change. They actively participated in creating the change they desired. Pause for a moment and consider what each one of the people I've mentioned, and others like them, have in common. What common threads run through their profiles? Apart from courage, determination and an unshakeable resolve to realise their vision, they lived on the edge of possibility not probability. And they stood up for something, something bigger than their own success. Their decisions and actions were guided by what is right and by love.

We have so much to learn from their actions and sacrifices and we owe them a great debt of gratitude. Because of their actions and sacrifices, freedom, individual dignity and hope were restored. Many of us today are spared the anguish, antagonism, injustice and annihilation faced daily by our great grand parents and their parents. Thanks to their legacy, we are all moved forward and each of us are able to breathe more easily.

I did everything I could so that you could reach as high as you could... I pressed into new territory. I took new ground. I pushed back the darkness. So take this baton of hope and rise higher than I ever thought possible. Change more than I ever thought could be changed. Take this power, this Gospel, this life-transforming truth and press it into the darkest, vilest places of the earth. Set prisoners free with it and never be afraid to try something new. Never be afraid to push the boundaries. Never be afraid to fail.

MALCOLM DUNCAN
Church and community founder and writer

- So, what or who is your enemy?
    - What action do you need to take right now?
    - What are you willing to sacrifice for victory? Are you willing to die for it? I truly believe that freedom, hope and peace are worth fighting and dying for on any given day.

There is no easy walk to freedom anywhere, and many of us will have to pass through the valley of the shadow of death again and again, before we reach the mountaintop of our desires.

NELSON MANDELA

- What bad habits do you have that may be holding you back from achieving your goals?
    - What can you do to overcome these habits?
- What bad habits do you have that may be affecting the quality of your personal relationships?
    - What steps can you take to overcome these habits?
- What distracts you from being present in your life?

Focused, determined champions win races. Distracted people become losers in the race of life.

JOHN DI LEMME
Business coach and motivational speaker

- List any distractions that sometimes stop you from really being present in the moment. Do you suffer from depression, dwelling on what's gone wrong in the past, anxiety, worrying about what could go wrong in the future or negativity?
- What action/s could you take to deal with your distractions? Photographing a breathtaking landscape? Cooking and sharing a sumptuous dinner with your loved ones? Watching a movie? Chatting to a therapist? Reading scriptures or words of wisdom? Meditation? What eases your distress is unique to your particular distraction and how you are uniquely wired. So take time to find your medicine and make sure you take it as much you need to.

- What fears are holding you back from your rainbow's end?

F-E-A-R has two meanings:

1. Forget Everything and Run

or

2. Face Everything and Rise.

The Choice is Yours.

UNKNOWN

  - List any fears that you sometimes allow to hold you back from really thinking big or which you have buried inside you, and have difficulty confronting. Are you afraid of failure, of success, of the negative voices that do not want you to stand out or to achieve your dreams?

  - What action can you to take right now to begin to overcome these fears? Because no matter how afraid you may be about something, it will never change unless you do something. Don't give your fear more power by fearing it. There is nothing you cannot conquer if you face it.

- List any situations that you don't feel very confident in. In these situations, you tend to feel uncomfortable and stuck.

  - What was happening at this time? Were you doubting yourself? Were you afraid?

  - How can you get past these situations in the future?

  - Do you need to speak to someone to help you work through them in the future? To really thrive in life, we need to learn how to overcome what makes us uncomfortable.

"Whether you prevail or fail, endure or die, depends more on what you do yourself than on what the world does to you."

JIM COLLINS
Business consultant and author

- List the situations that you really feel confident, alive and vibrant in. In these situations, everything you do flows.

  - What was happening at this time?

- List any stereotypes you encounter.

  - How can you undermine these stereotypes? People's stereotype of you can form their lasting opinion of you. So you need to learn how to undermine any such stereotype. Never default to a stereotype. You may not be able to control some of the stereotypes that may exist about you, because most stereotypes are down to others' prejudices. However, you can undermine it by acting contrary to the stereotype and always presenting yourself at your very best. For example, one of the key obstacles some people face in business is not their competitor, but the stereotypes others have of them. One of the ways to manage this is to take a moment before any important meeting and ask yourself, 'How are they likely to stereotype me? Does my appearance reinforce this stereotype?' If your answer is, 'Yes', dress contrary to the stereotype to undermine it. Conversely, you can change the context of the stereotype by adopting it as part of your brand and making it attractive, and along the way, perhaps causing a paradigm change.

- Think of your target audience.

  - How do they stereotype you or how are they likely to stereotype you?

  - How can you undermine this stereotype?

"If something stands between you and your success - move it. Never be denied."

DWAYNE JOHNSON
Actor and wrestler

- What can you do in the future to ensure that you always present yourself confidently, without compromising any of your values or aspirations?

- Do you recognise perfectionism as one of your barriers?

    - If so, list three things that you've been putting off until conditions are much better.

    - List three things you can do right now to move these situations forward.

EXERCISE 3

- Identify one of your most important intentions relating to your personal presentation. Please, write it down.

Example: I want to always express myself boldly and without any inhibitions. My goal is to create a distinctive, compelling and enduring personal brand that inspires and invigorates others, attracts opportunities and...

- Write a description of the person you want to become.

    - What do you need to do to become this person?

    - Can you commit to acting like this person from now on?

You've got to write the storyline for your future. Who you are today is the sum of all the decisions you've made and your current storyline. If you want a change, you must change your story. Yes, it is in our hands to define our future. Get a vision of your best self and work hard until you become it.

Raise your gaze, Look skyward
It's obvious you're great
You're a champion.

MONALISA

MONALISA

CHAPTER

4. CELEBRATING YOUR UNIQUE QUALITIES

One must have the daring to accept oneself as a bundle of possibilities and undertake the most interesting game in the world - making the most of one's best.

HARRY EMERSON FOSDICK

Baptist and Presbyterian minister

I can't tell you how often, during an initial consultation, a client asks me, "*What do I need to change to look great? What do I need to change to be a great photographer, actor, entrepreneur, consultant, writer, speaker, host... ? What type of image do you think I need?*"

Wrong questions! One of the first things I explain to my clients is that as an Image Maker, my job is not to change you or to tell you what would make you look or be great. What makes one person look great or to be great at his or her job is different for the next person. You do not need to change anything to look or to be great at what you do. You are *who you are for a reason. Who you are* is where your power lies, where your magic lies. You can always refine or develop yourself and be the best you possibly can be, but you must never fundamentally change what makes you unique - your talents, skills, values and the way you see the world.

"Hide not your talents. They for use were made. What's a sundial in the shade?"

BENJAMIN FRANKLIN
American polymath and diplomat

You're you. There is no one else like you. You have 46 chromosomes: 23 from your mother and 23 from your father, and so much nuance. Your makeup of atoms, molecules and genes are arranged in a distinctive way from anyone else. The chances of your parents creating another child exactly like you is one in a trillion. You have a unique set of talents, abilities and potentials that nobody else has. Because of this, nobody's path in life is the same as yours. There are gifts that only you can give, stories that only you tell, and dreams that only you can fulfil. Recognising your unique qualities and devoting your life to developing them to their full potential will help you to operate at your very best. You become great by following the path of your greatest talents and abilities.

I can't possibly tell you what type of image you need. I don't conjure images. My job is to help you develop an image that fits perfectly into the context of your personal brand - your unique qualities and aspirations. Through a series of detailed questions and exercises that focus on what makes you unique, I will help you find out *who you are* by clarifying:

- what your unique qualities are;
- your goals, aspirations and expectations; and
- how you can use your unique qualities to achieve your goals and to become your very best self.

Only then can we - you and I - build an image that fits your personal brand perfectly.

Many of us are only using a fraction of our qualities. My goal in this chapter is to encourage you to reveal and embrace all your unique qualities. There are things in each of us that must come out. I want you

"If you can't be a highway, then just be a trail,
If you can't be the sun, be a star;
It isn't by the size that you win or you fail."

DOUGLAS MALLOCH
Be the Best of Whatever You Are

to look inside you. Listen to that unstoppable voice in your head and heart that is constantly demanding expression and give it definition. Life really flows and attracts greatness when you fully recognise, embrace and develop your unique qualities. It is what makes us stand out that inspires us to write, to paint, to compose beautiful symphonies, to lead a nation from fear and poverty to freedom or to provide solutions to the unique problems that our humanity faces daily.

EXERCISE 4

To get you started in identifying your unique qualities, please take a comprehensive look at yourself - your talents, abilities, what turns you on - and answer the following questions honestly and rigorously. Acknowledge your limitations. Pretending to be something you're not, would be simply a waste of your time. Being positive, tough and brutally honest with yourself during this self analysis is the difference between developing a great and compelling personal brand and a mediocre one. To get the most from this exercise, please write down your answers.

- What do you like to do? What do you love - your passion? What are your quirks? Don't make value judgements about whether it is important or not. Don't dismiss anything.

- What are you good at? I am asking for your proven talents - the things you know you are good at, and have proven that you are good at.

- What do you need to feel fulfilled? Where do you want to add value?

You have to know what sparks the light in you, so that you, in your own way, can illuminate the world.

OPRAH WINFREY

- Are there any commonalities between what you like to do, what you love, your quirks and what you are good at? If there are, you are well on your way. If there aren't, you have a choice. You can:

  - Look at what you like to do, what you love and your quirks in greater detail, identifying the key skills you would need to acquire to become great at them. How and where can you develop these skills? How can you use these skills to meet your needs and add value to the lives of others?

  - Or, you may need to concentrate on developing and refining what you are good at, working on your proven talents to turn them into valuable abilities.

Whatever your choice is, it takes years and years of practice and commitment to become great at anything you do that involves a skill or expertise. The psychologist Dr. K. Anders Ericsson says that it takes 10,000 hours - 20 hours for 50 weeks a year for 10 years - to become excellent in any chosen skill. There is a school of thought that argues that 10,000 hours of deliberate practice on its own does not guarantee world-class performance or expertise, but rather it's the quality of those 10,000 hours that matters. So, as also recommended by Ericsson, outstanding performance requires practice - deliberate practice, refinement and more practice. You may need the help of coaches and mentors to develop, refine or enhance your talents and abilities.

Your true success in life begins only when you make the commitment to become excellent at what you do. Every study of high achieving men and women proves that greatness in life is only possible when you become outstanding at your chosen field.

BRIAN TRACY

Author and motivational speaker

- What are the three things that make you memorable? Many times, people hesitate in answering this question, because they don't believe that they have many memorable attributes. Wrong! Please work with me. You may start by standing in front of a mirror. Think of the last person that made you smile. What did they say or do? Now, are you smiling again? Describe your smile. Is it memorable? Because every smile is. What are your cheekbones doing during this smile? Are there dimples on them? And your eyes, are they twinkling? Look at your hair, your skin, your lips... I could go on. The things that make us memorable flow smoothly into each other. You only have to pay attention.

- What do people always compliment you on?

- What knowledge, abilities, personal characteristics and life experiences do you have that add value to the lives of your friends and family?

  - What promise do you deliver on consistently to your friends and family? Companionship, understanding, unconditional love, generosity, consideration, compassion, thoughtfulness, loyalty, guidance, patience...?

  - How could you add more value to the lives of your friends and family?

"Everything has beauty, but not every one sees it."

CONFUCIUS
Philosopher

- What value do you add to the lives of your clients or customers?
  - What promise do you deliver on consistently to your clients or customers? Professional excellence, innovation excellence, great craftsmanship, integrity, service, comfort, individual dignity...?
  - How could you add more value to the lives of your clients or customers?
- What value do you add to the lives of people in your community; your neighbours, professional groups, religious groups, and so on?
  - What promise do you deliver on consistently to this group? Leadership, integrity, individual dignity, service, friendship...?
  - How could you add more value to the lives of people in your community?
- What is most important to you in your personal relationships? Friendship, commitment, shared values and interests, mutual respect, unconditional love... ?
- What is most important to you in your business relationships? Trust, dependability, honesty, flexibility... ?
- What drives you in business or work? Money, power, making a contribution, feeling valued... ?

"No matter how potent your talents are, they remain to be out of use until you take time to develop them to their optimum level. This calls for preparation. Through preparation, personal branding, consistent exposure and productive connections, you set up a condition for your dreams to flourish and bear fruits!"

ISRAELMORE AYIVOR
Writer and self improvement motivator

The collection of qualities you've identified in this exercise are your brand assets. If there are too many qualities on your list, it may be difficult for others to remember them. You may need to choose a handful of the key qualities from this list that you want to be known for by your world. These are the qualities that will give your personal brand its distinctive power. They represent the value you provide and are the foundation on which you build your personal brand. The key to creating a successful personal brand is to play to your talents. Soaring against the grain of your unique qualities will only lead to frustration and mediocrity.

Your talents are your raw materials and you have to put every ounce of them to use. However, whatever set of talents you are gifted, some assembly will be required. As I mentioned earlier, for talent to yield high performance and enduring success, it must be accompanied by focused, excruciating, long-term hard work, without which the world will be denied of the value you could have contributed.

Have the courage to be You.

MONALISA

MONALISA

CHAPTER

5. COMPONENTS OF YOUR PERSONAL BRAND

Well orchestrated brands have depth and richness. They are like personalities, in that the best of them are made interesting and beautiful by a unique blend of interesting and beautiful component parts. It is only in the harmony of the whole that the brand lives.

STEVE YASTROW
Author

There are seven main components to your personal brand: One-thing

5.1. YOUR ONE WORD

This is the single word that sums up all that you aim for in life. This word will sum up the outcome that all your possible audiences will expect from you in everything you do or anything you are involved in. Living this one word means that you will be intentional about demonstrating it in all that you do and all that you are.

5.2. YOUR WHO YOU ARE AND WHAT YOU DO STATEMENTS

- *Who you are* is a statement of who you are at your core. *Who you are* is where your power and magic lies. It embraces everything about you. Everything you need to excel, to be unique, to be innovative, is within *who you are*.

- *What you do* is the value you add to the lives of your target audience. It is the difference you make. And it is part of *who you are*. There isn't a separation. The key questions to ask yourself as you construct your *what you do* statement are:

  - Is it clear and simple?

  - Does it inspire confidence that you are focused enough to master and invest in it?

  - Is it focused enough for others to recall it as your speciality?

  - Does it convey power?

5.3. YOUR TARGET AUDIENCE

Who you serve and who you want to serve in the future. This includes your target audience and all your possible future target audience for each area of your life and how you bring or will bring value to their lives. The target audience for:

- your work: your clients, customers, business associates, coworkers and so on.

- your personal life: the people you love and care most about.

- your community: your professional associations, religious groups, local groups and so on.

5.4. YOUR PURPOSE AND VISION

- **Your purpose** is your *why you do it* statement. This is the fixed purpose around which everything you do in your life revolves. It is at the core of everything you do. A few questions you may ask yourself to help you bring your purpose into focus are:

  - What are you determined to achieve in your life? This is your true purpose in life - to heal the sick, to create beauty, to create communities, to love others, to help the lost...

  - What difference do you want to make in the lives of your target audience?

  - What do you want to be remembered for?

- **Your vision**. This is your vision of *who you want to become* or *what you want to achieve in your life*. It is your *where* question - where you are going? Start by drawing a detailed picture of who you want to become, what you want to achieve in your life and where you want to be. Refine it again and again, until it clearly tells the story of your intentions for your greater future. Your vision empowers your purpose. It helps you to see clearly where you are going clearly, motivating you to work towards your desired end.

5.5. YOUR CORE VALUES

What you stand for. You need to be very clear about the values that guide your decisions and behaviour. Make sure that they are more than just mere words. Some key questions to help you ensure that you get these right are:

- Is this value genuine and relevant to your brand? How is it important to your brand?
- Does the value contribute to the uniqueness of your brand? Is it differentiating?
- Is the value compelling enough to keep you motivated to stand for and by it?
- Is this value achievable? Are you confident that you can commit to living by this value and demonstrating it in your actions 24/7/365 and for the longer-term?
- Does the value tap into the needs, concerns and aspirations of your target audience?
- Can you communicate this value clearly to people?

5.6. YOUR BRAND MANTRA

This is a simple, short, clear, vivid, memorable and powerful phrase or sentence of about two to seven words. It needs to capture the spirit, uniqueness and raison d'être of your personal brand. It is an essential part of the DNA of your personal brand, forming the foundation and guiding principle of all your future decisions and actions. This is a sentence or phrase that you uniquely own and keep referring back to whenever you have to make an important decision or choice, such as what types of projects you will get involved in, what types of causes you will support or champion, or what types of investment you will make. It will guide how you will show up to your personal, professional or business engagements and the level of commitment that you bring.

Come up with something that is deeply and truly meaningful to you, inspiring and motivating you to action, resonating with your target audience and setting your personal brand boundaries, to stop you from over-reaching them. It should define where you can and can't go with your personal brand by being explicit about what it is or isn't.

This will be your guide for living your personal brand, 24/7/365, and it will keep you on the right course for decades to come. Your brand mantra is internally facing and not for external use. It will serve as a constant reminder of who you are, what you do and why you do it, what you stand for, your core values, your purpose and vision and who you serve. This sentence or phrase is there to:

- inspire and motivate you;
- differentiate you from other personal brands; and
- keep your personal brand message consistent and your brand on track by guiding your decision-making, keeping you focused on what is important to you and your target audience.

"All great masters are chiefly distinguished by the power of adding a second, a third, and perhaps a fourth step in a continuous line. Many a man had taken the first step. With every additional step you enhance immensely the value of your first."

RALPH WALDO EMERSON
Poet, philosopher and essayist

5.7. YOUR TAGLINE

Your tagline is a simple, short, clear, vivid, memorable and powerful phrase or sentence of about two to seven words that communicates your personal brand mantra to your target audience. It is an external expression of your personal brand mantra. It captures the essence of your personal brand's promise to your target audience. Unlike your personal brand mantra, which is internally facing to inspire and motivate you, your tagline is externally facing to inspire and motivate your target audience, inviting them to take an interest in you, your personal brand and the value it provides.

Like your brand mantra, it represents *what you stand for*. This sentence will tell all your possible target audiences what it is like to be around you and get them interested in you and you're personal brand, its message and the value you provide. It will represent:

- who you are at your core;
- your vision for your life - the essence of what you want to achieve in this world; and
- how you want to make a difference, not only in your work, but in your relationships and every other facet of your life - the way you want to touch others.

We will look at each of the above components in greater detail in Chapter 8.

The only way I can be,
Is to be me.

MONALISA

MONALISA

CHAPTER

6. CHECKLIST FOR SUCCESS

The keys to brand success are self-definition, transparency, authenticity and accountability.

SIMON MAINWARING

Branding consultant and advertising creative director

The principles of marketing people are very different. The best way to market your personal brand is to be such a stand out that other people will generate a buzz for you. To stand out, your personal brand must be:

- ***Clear and simple:*** your personal brand should communicate a clear and simple message, because you are selling to the overwhelmed - and they crave simplicity and clarity. So edit and tell your story clearly and simply. Your credo should be, "*Less is so much more*".

- ***Unique and distinctive:*** being distinctive and outstanding in some way is hugely important in personal branding. The more focused and unique your personal brand is, the more powerful it will be over your lifetime. To be unique, your personal brand must say something different and should be as distinctive as your fingerprint. You need to find a way to tell such a distinctive and compelling story that it resonates with your target audience.

- ***Meaningful:*** your brand message must be based on a clear purpose and must be meaningful to you and your target audience.

- ***Compelling and Inviting:*** you must use compelling prose to describe your message, not clichés. Your personal brand should be so positive and compelling that it inspires and invigorates others and invites opportunities.

- ***Enduring:*** your brand will endure if it provides real and lasting value to everyone associated with it.

- ***Authentic:*** great personal brands are authentic. People have learnt they are credible and have come to trust these brands to be what they say they are. Who they are and what they say are integrated with what they do.

- ***Vivid and Memorable:*** a vivid representation of your brand in its packaging will help you convey the meaning of your brand visually and clearly. People often forget words, but they notice and remember images, especially vivid and extraordinary ones. So, don't settle for average. Your presentation and visual identity - your logo and any other design elements - that visually and vividly express what your brand means to the world must stand out. It's a crowded world, and this helps people remember you clearly.

Success is the progressive realisation of a worthy ideal. Therefore, who succeeds? The only person who succeeds is the person who is progressively realising a worthy ideal. Such a person says, "I'm going to become this", and then begins to work toward becoming it.

EARL NIGHTINGALE
Motivational speaker and author

PART II

If you had one last job to do –
What would it be?

MONALISA

CHAPTER

7. THE PERSONAL BRANDING FORMULA

If you want to create an outstanding, compelling and extraordinary personal brand, create an outstanding, compelling and extraordinary you. The best way to create an outstanding brand is to provide an outstanding value in everything you do. Your target audience will know this by observing your actions and by recognising the value you add to their lives.

Every powerful brand is characterised by a logically constructed set of brand-building steps. The personal branding formula in this chapter is a blueprint that any one can use to build a distinctive, compelling and enduring personal brand. The formula can be distilled into four key steps. We will be looking at these steps in the following pages.

Your time is limited, so don't waste it living someone else's life. Don't be trapped by dogma – which is living with the results of other people's thinking. Don't let the noise of other's opinions drown out your own inner voice. And most important, have the courage to follow your heart and intuition. They somehow already know what you truly want to become. Everything else is secondary.

STEVE JOBS

Entrepreneur, inventor and co-founder of Apple

"The heart of a brand is not slick packaging, artifice, cleverness, or polish. The heart of a brand is the truth."

HARRY BECKWITH
Author, speaker and teacher

THE PERSONAL BRANDING FORMULA	
THE FOUR PERSONAL BRAND-BUILDING STEPS	
STEP I	Define and develop your personal brand: • your one word and statements; • your target audience; • your purpose and vision; • your values; • your brand mantra; and • your tagline
STEP II	Package your personal brand: • your name; • your personal story; • your visual identity; and • your personal and business presentation
STEP III	Distribute your personal brand any where and every where that you interact with your target audience - home, studio or office, website, social networks, and others
STEP IV	Live your personal brand, 24/7/365

MONALISA

CHAPTER

8. STEP 1: DEFINE AND DEVELOP YOUR PERSONAL BRAND

I have decided to be more than just a "tick tock" kind of clock. When time drags, I can make it fly. To give a second chance, my seconds spin backwards. And imagine, if I made precious moments less momentary. In the end, we have a choice. Do we settle for ordinary, or do we strive to be made of more?

GUINNESS 'MADE OF MORE' COMMERCIAL, 2013

It's time to build your personal brand. The one you need for your greater future. ***A personal brand that is such a stand out that it creates a buzz for you. A personal brand that will leave a legacy.*** Remember,

Your brand is the truth about you, well told.

OLD ADVERTISING SLOGAN

So what's your truth? Make sure you tell it well.

Let's get started!

EXERCISE 5

Please answer the following questions positively, honestly and rigorously. Make sure you write down your answers, because you will need to refine, develop and refer to your answers many times in the future.

DESCRIBE YOURSELF IN ONE WORD - This is the single word that sums up *who you are* and all that you aim for in life. Reducing *who you ar*e into one word will force you to become crystal clear about your essence. This one word will sum up your reputation – *your personal brand* - and it will be the backbone of how you live your personal life, business life, useful also for your personal publicity campaign. You will personify this word, live up to it, deliver on it 24/7/365, every time you package yourself, every time you walk into a room, in every conversation, in the way you perform every task and in the way you deliver on your commitments. This word will sum up the outcome that all your possible audiences will expect from you in everything you do or anything you are involved in. Living this one word means that you will be intentional about demonstrating it in all that you do and all that you are.

I recently watched a BBC documentary into the private life and achievements of the eccentric music performer and producer Will.i.am - William Adams - in which the actress and author Joanna Lumley spent time with Will.i.am in his home town of Los Angeles, to shed light on the man behind the global brand, Will.i.am and his impoverished upbringing in the projects of Los Angeles. At one revealing moment, Joanna asked:

Joanna Lumley: *If you had to think of one word that's most important to you, or that sums you up, or that would be kind of, like a beacon, what would it be?*

Will.i.am: *Will! To have will ... to have determination. strength, courage - Will.*

He did not have to think about his one word. It was very clear that this word had been guiding his actions for a long time.

So, if for example, your one word is *excellence,* you will be compelled to bring excellence into everything you do. You will always show up brilliantly, dressed appropriately, prepared and ready to exceed expectations. The word 'mediocrity' will automatically flee from your vocabulary and life. And if your one word is *elegance*, you will have to denounce the caprices of fashion and become the very epitome of style. You will be devoted to elegance. Your clothes, accessories, your whole demeanour, the way you carry yourself, the way you move and the way you relate to others, will be imbued with timelessly effortless style and luxurious austerity. The word 'sloven' will automatically flee from your vocabulary and life.

- Now write down your one word.
- Are you going to be able to *look this word*, *act this word* and *be this word* 24/7/365?
- Is this word what you need for your greater future?
- Is this the clear and positive word that you want people to use to describe you?

EXERCISE 6

Put words to the following statements:

YOUR WHO YOU ARE, WHAT YOU DO and WHY IT

MATTERS statements - You may refer to Chapter 5, Section 5.2, to see my previous explanation of **WHO YOU ARE** and **WHAT YOU DO** statements.

Be positive concerning who you are and what you do. The world is not hungry for mediocrity. As the saying goes, ***"You are what you think you are'.*** **WHO YOU ARE** goes beyond your job or title. We are looking for ***clear, positive and compelling statements that will come to mind when people think of you.*** **WHAT YOU DO** is the value you add to the lives of your target audience - the difference you make. And it should:

- be clear, simple and convey power.
- inspire confidence that you are focused enough to master and invest in it?
- be focused enough for others to recall it as your speciality?

WHAT DO YOU NOT WANT TO DO?

We must overcome the notion that we must be ordinary... It robs you of the chance to be extraordinary, and leads you to the mediocre.

UTA HAGEN
Actress and drama teacher

EXERCISE 7

YOUR PURPOSE AND YOUR VISION

There is no greater agony than bearing an untold story inside you.

MAYA ANGELOU
Author, poet and actress

A. WHAT IS YOUR PURPOSE? What is the fixed purpose around which everything you do in your life revolves? Please note that I said *fixed purpose*. This is because your purpose does not significantly change over your lifetime. Of course it may expand as you grow, but its main focus hardly ever changes. It is not an action. Your purpose dictates the agenda for your life. It motivates your actions and your actions are how you achieve it. Working through the following questions will help you bring your purpose into focus. Please write down your answers.

What really matters to you?

- What are you determined to achieve in your life? This is your true purpose in life. It may be: to heal the sick, to create art, to educate women, to tell stories, to love others, to help the lost, to entertain the world... ?
- What difference do you want to make in the lives of your target audience?
- What do you want to be famous for?

"This is the true joy in life, the being used for a purpose recognised by yourself as a mighty one; the being a force of nature instead of a feverish, selfish little clod of ailments and grievances complaining that the world will not devote itself to making you happy. I want to be thoroughly used up when I die, for the harder I work the more I live."

GEORGE BERNARD SHAW

Once you have a purpose that you are willing to dedicate your life to, it will unleash a level of passion, motivation and inner strength that you've never experienced before. Next, work through the following questions to get a better understanding of this purpose.

- What frightens you most about this purpose?
- How can you use your daily activities to serve this purpose?
- What kind of challenges do you think you'd face as you begin working toward this purpose?
- What resources can you draw on to help you overcome these challenges?

B. WHAT IS YOUR GRAND VISION OF WHO YOU WANT TO BECOME or WHAT YOU WANT TO ACHIEVE IN YOUR LIFE?

This is your where question: *where you are going*? It requires you to step out of your comfort zone and really think big.

- Where would you like to be in ten years' time from now?

Note that you will never rise above the image you have in your mind in any area of your life. So, please be your most inspired, dynamic, and creative self. Don't put a limit on your imagination. A modest vision will only inspire mediocre actions and a mediocre future. The first step in creating the greater future you want is to envision it. Imagine that you have a blank canvas. Please paint a grand picture for your future. Remember we are creating a personal brand that is such a standout that it creates a buzz for you. So you should aim beyond what you think you are capable of. Nothing you can envision is impossible. And even if you don't hit that desired mark exactly, you'd be far beyond where you started and much closer to your dream.

"It may never be mine,
The loaf or the kiss or the kingdom,
Because of beseeching.
But I know that my hand
Is an arm's length nearer the sky
For reaching."

EDWIN QUARLES
Petition

For more inspiration for painting your vision, please see the following **advertisement** once placed as a public service in the **Wall Street Journal** by the **United Technologies Corporation of Hartford, Connecticut.**

Aim So High You'll Never Be Bored

The greatest waste of our natural resources

is the number of people

who never achieve their potential.

Get out of that slow lane.

Shift into that fast lane.

If you think you can't you won't.

If you think you can, there's a good chance you will.

Even making the effort

will make you feel like a new person.

Reputations are made by searching

for things that can't be done

and doing them.

Aim low: boring.

Aim high: soaring.

EXERCISE 8

WHO IS YOUR TARGET AUDIENCE? - Who do you serve and who do you want to serve in the future? Who is your target audience and future target audience for:

- Your work?
  - Consider the needs, concerns and perspectives of this audience.
  - What do they need that you are currently providing?
  - What do they need that you are not currently providing? Can you provide for these needs?
  - How could you bring more value into the lives of this audience?
  - What do you want this audience to think, know, feel and say about you?
- Your personal relationships?
  - Consider the needs, concerns and perspectives of this audience.
  - What do they need that you are currently providing?
  - What do they need that you are not currently providing? Can you provide for these needs?
  - How could you bring more value into the lives of this audience?
  - What do you want this audience to think, know, feel and say about you?

- Your communities?
    - Consider the needs, concerns and perspectives of this audience.
    - What do they need that you are currently providing?
    - What do they need that you are not currently providing? Can you provide for these needs?
    - How could you bring more value into the lives of this audience?
    - What do you want this audience to think, know, feel and say about you?

EXERCISE 9

DEFINE YOUR VALUES – what you stand for. These are the set of values that guide your decisions and behaviour. Asking yourself the following questions and answering them honestly will help you ensure that you set real values that will enhance your brand message:

- Is this value genuine and relevant to my brand? How is it important to my brand?
- Does this value contribute to the uniqueness of my brand? Is it differentiating?
- Is this value compelling enough to keep me motivated to stand for and by it?
- Is this value achievable? Am I confident that I can commit to living by this value and demonstrating it in my actions 24/7/365 and for the long-term?

- Does this value tap into the needs, concerns and aspirations of my target audience?
- Can I communicate this value clearly to people?

EXERCISE 10

DEVELOP YOUR BRAND MANTRA. Draft a simple, short, clear, vivid, memorable and powerful phrase or sentence of about two to seven words. This sentence should capture the spirit of your personal brand, what is unique about you and the raison d'être of your personal brand. It's that secret formula that colours your every action - how you live your personal brand, your personal, professional or business decisions, your personal publicity, packaging, and so on.

This is a sentence or phrase that you will uniquely own, and will keep coming back to whenever you have to make an important decision or choice, such as which types of projects, you will get involved in, what types of causes you will support or champion, what types of investment you will make. It will guide how you show up to your personal, professional or business engagements and the level of commitment that you will bring. Come up with something that is deeply and truly meaningful to you, inspiring and motivating you to action, resonating with your target audience and setting your personal brand boundaries, to stop you from over-reaching them. It should define where you can and can't go with your personal brand by being explicit about what it is or isn't.

This will be your guide for living your personal brand, 24/7/365, and it will keep you on the right course for decades to come. Your brand mantra is internally facing and not for external use. It will serve as a constant reminder of who you are, what you do and why you do it, what you stand for, your core values, your purpose and vision and who you serve. This sentence or phrase will:

- inspire and motivate you;
- differentiate you from other people and personal brands; and
- keep your personal brand message consistent and on track by guiding your decision making, keeping you focused on what is important to you and your target audience.

Four classic examples of brand mantras that I find really inspiring are:

- *Chanel's* brand mantra: *simplicity, elegance and independence.*

The most courageous act is still to think for yourself. Aloud.

GABRIELLE '*COCO*' CHANEL

Fashion designer and founder of the Chanel brand

- The Chanel company was founded by the formidable, iconoclastic and personal branding legend, Gabrielle '*Coco*' Chanel, who injected her innate elegance, life experience and game changing creativity into the Chanel brand. Chanel wanted women to be independent and to wear clothes for themselves, not for the pleasure of men. She reflected these values and her aesthetic judgments in her classic, corset free and alluring garments, which revitalised and changed the look of fashion forever. Her brand mantra was the basic driver of her lines and looks.

- Apple's Brand Mantra: *think different*

I would rather gamble on our vision than make a 'me, too' product.

STEVE JOBS
Entrepreneur, inventor and co-founder of Apple

Apple is the American multinational corporation that designs and sells consumer electronics, computer software and personal computers that used to be led by Steve Jobs. All products and activities associated with Apple have to be different and they achieve this by offering the latest technology in laptops, computers, software and exceptional customer experience in portable media players in very beautiful and innovative designs.

- Ritz-Carlton's Brand Mantra: *ladies and gentlemen serving ladies and gentlemen*

Our ladies and gentlemen might not have the wealth, knowledge, or education of our guests, but they have the same values.

SIMON COOPER
President and CEO, the Ritz-Carlton Hotel Company, 2001-10

The Ritz hotel is known worldwide as the leading luxury and most admired lodging brand for its outstanding customer service. Many successful brands including Apple were influenced by this lifestyle brand's service model of anticipating the customer's expressed and unexpressed needs, when designing their customer support systems.

The Ritz brand's focus is on staff engagement, empowerment and reward, and customer outcomes rather than systems. The Ritz brand mantra is rigorously adhered to in its gold standards and this is reflected in its written service strategy and its remarkable staff engagement and empowerment policy. This policy entrusts every single staff member with the option of spending up to £1,500 on a guest, per incident, without approval from their general manager. It also rewards staff for exceptional service. The impressive result of their brand mantra is their growing loyal customer base, absolutely married to the Ritz. Also, the Ritz has the highest level of staff loyalty and retention in the hospitality industry.

- Nike's Brand Mantra: *authentic athletic performance*

Nike's brand Mantra put a particular emphasis on maintaining 'authenticity' by which we also meant integrity and purity, front and centre. All images and associations with our products had to be real, not contrived.

SCOTT BEDBURY
A New Brand World

According to Scott Bedbury, the marketing expert at Nike in the 1980s, the term ***brand mantra*** was coined during his time at Nike. Scott said in his book, *A New Brand World*, that as stated in Nike's brand mantra, all products and activities associated with Nike had to be authentic, athletic, not leisurely, and they must exude world class performance. Finally, all Nike products had to meet the demands of the world's finest athletes, even though such athletes represented only a small part of Nike's total business.

This mantra continues to endure because it effectively differentiates Nike from its competitors, inspiring and focusing employees on Nike's core values, its target market and what really matters to Nike.

EXERCISE 11

CREATE A TAGLINE THAT REPRESENTS WHAT YOU STAND FOR. Once you are clear and firm on your brand mantra, it is time to compose your tagline - a simple phrase or sentence that allows people to define you the way want to be seen. Your tagline is an external expression of your personal brand mantra. It captures the essence of your personal brand's promise to your target audience. Unlike your personal brand mantra, which is internally facing and is there to inspire and motivate you, your tagline is externally facing and is there to inspire and motivate your target audience and to invite them to take an interest in you, your personal brand and the value it provides. In Exercise 10 above, we briefly looked at Nike's brand mantra - *Authentic Athletic Performance*. The external expression of Nike's brand mantra, which is better known than its brand mantra, because it is externally facing and intended to inspire and motivate Nike's target audience, is *Just Do It*.

So your tagline is a simple, short, vivid, memorable and powerful phrase or sentence of about two to seven words that communicates your personal brand mantra to your target audience. Like your brand mantra, it represents *what you stand for*. Come up with something that you'll never tire of saying or hearing. You will live with and hear this phrase for decades to come, so take your time to come up with something that will be there for your greater future. Something that is deeply and truly meaningful to you, resonates with your target audience and, like Nike's *Just Do It*, inspires and motivates your target audience to action. This sentence will tell all your possible target audiences what it is like to be around you and get them interested in you and you're personal brand, its message and the value you provide. It will represent:

- who you are at your core;
- your vision for your life - the essence of what you want to achieve in this world - and
- how you want to make a difference, not only in your work, but in your relationships and every other facet of your life - the way you want to touch others.

Four classic examples of memorable taglines are:

SOME MEMORABLE TAGLINES	
Susan Wiggs	Laugh. Cry. Dream. Read.
City of Las Vegas	What happens in Vegas, stays in Vegas
L'Oreal	Because I'm worth it
Nike	Just do it

Make yours equally memorable.

"If you can dream it, you can do it."

WALT DISNEY

Business magnate, animator and screenwriter

EXERCISE 12

Visualise yourself in front of a huge and mixed audience at a leukaemia charity event you've organised. You are about to deliver a speech to ask for donations for this charity and to raise awareness of some of the recent issues surrounding leukaemia - a cause that is very dear to your heart. Your audience includes many of the most powerful and influential people in politics, business and entertainment; and their children. Some of your audience have undergone or are currently having leukaemia therapy. There are television cameras positioned to broadcast the evening's event to an even broader viewing audience around the world.

This is the first filter that your audience will put you through when considering whether:

- they will associate with you;
- they connect or can connect with you and your charity in some way;
- they want to really dip their hands into their pockets to support your very worthy cause.

Keep your speech simple and straightforward. Make sure the seven-year old sitting in the front row can understand you. Start with the story of your personal brand. Make sure you talk about your aspirations, the difference you want to make and the value you and your audience can bring to this charity and the world around you.

"Everyone has inside of him a piece of good news. The good news is that you don't know how great you can be! How much you can love! What you can accomplish! And what your potential is!"

ANNELIES 'ANNE' FRANK
One of the Jewish victims of the Holocaust

You may need several hours for the above exercises. It may take you up to a week, a month or several months to find your word, your statements, the brand mantra and tagline that works for you. The important thing is to really think about each statement and make sure that each element's inclusion in your personal brand will help meet the demands of your greater future.

Style is about individuality.

MONALISA

CHAPTER

9. STEP II: PACKAGE YOUR PERSONAL BRAND

The celebrity look can be created; the sound of intelligence can be learned. Do these two things and you have the packaging for a powerful personal brand.

JAY JESSUP

Fame 101

Packaging is the second step of the personal branding formula. A distinctive packaging is your main weapon for illustrating, illuminating and bringing your personal brand to life. It communicates the message of your personal brand in visual terms. At step one, you defined who you are and who you want to be. Step two is about creating a look for your personal brand. It's about skilfully translating who you defined into an eternal packaging and style. Your *brand packaging* includes:

- your *name* and how it is perceived by your target audience;
- your *personal story* - the key story or stories that define who you are today;
- your *visual identity* - your logo and the associated design elements that generate recognition for you; and
- your *personal and business presentation* - how you package and present yourself and your business.

This does not just package you. It is your way of making yourself and the unique attributes of your personal brand seen, and a critical part of your target audience's experience of you. Your *brand packaging* reflects and shows the qualities of your personal brand. You as the protagonist of your brand will live these qualities 24/7/365. A distinctive packaging sells your brand and gives you authenticity. The wrong packaging will undermine your brand. So make sure that your brand packaging projects your story vividly and leaves an indelible impression. Your packaging should be *distinctive, simple, clear and brand-obsessive.*

The key elements to consider when designing your packaging are as follows.

9.1. YOUR NAME

What's in a name? That which we call a rose
By any other name would smell as sweet.

WILLIAM SHAKESPEARE
Romeo and Juliet, Act 2, Scene 2

Many of us are influenced by the title of a book, a piece of music or a movie. As such, people form a distinct impression when they hear your name. Your name has an impact on how you see yourself and therefore is highly influential in the forming of your character and how you are perceived. Because your name announces your identity, influences how you feel about yourself and how others feel about you and respond to you, no work on image building would be complete without ensuring that your name makes a positive impression on your target audience and that you are proud of it.

The right name lights up, propels and lifts up a person to extraordinary heights. Hollywood film studios' image makers understood the importance of a person's name and the big difference a name can make to an individual's personal brand and packaging. In Hollywood, plain Norma Jean Mortenson became Marilyn Monroe, Sophia Villani Scicolone became Sophia Loren, Margarita Carmen Cansino became Rita Hayworth, Issur Danielovitch became Kirk Douglas, Archibald Leach became Cary Grant and Maurice Micklewhite became Michael Caine. A fleet of Hollywood's top image consultants, beauty therapists, hair professionals, makeup artists, cosmetic dentists, fashion designers, tailors and stylists, voice, speech and acting coaches all joined forces to polish the hell out of these actors to what we were finally presented with on the big screen. The result is that each of these actors considerably increased their perceived value, earning power and attracted greater opportunities, far beyond those of their peers. The main lesson here is that your name and the rest of your packaging is a vital asset with an impact on what you are trying to accomplish and how you are perceived, which ultimately determines your acceptance.

As your name does affect your personal brand and image and influences your level of acceptance by your target audience, it is vital that you ensure that you are not the victim of your name. Your name should work for, not against you.

So what is the best name for your personal brand?

The one thing I want to leave my children is an honorable name.

THEODORE ROOSEVELT

Twenty-sixth President of the United States, 1901-09

The rule of thumb is generally, to stay away from using initials, which are more a tool of convenience rather than of the heart. One word is much easier to remember than two or three words. The best names are those that reflect your personal brand and personality. Such names are also distinctive, memorable, confident, going a long way towards telling your story and promoting you and your activities. Unusual names also work well because they get you noticed and remembered. However, you should definitely consider a name change if your name:

- does not reflect your personal brand;
- has a negative, vulgar, objectionable or inappropriate meaning or overtones in the language of some of your target audience that is hindering you in your personal and business relationships; and
- is too long or difficult to pronounce (eleven letters and four syllables is the recommended maximum).

For example, the psychological thriller, *The Omen* released in 1976 and its remake, *The Omen: 666* released in 2006, both starring the demonic child *Damien*, sealed the fate and changed the meaning of the name Damien. Since both films came out, the name Damien, which used to mean *one who tames*, became known as *the devil's spawn* or *the child of Satan*. Today, not many Christian parents will name their child Damien, because of this change in perception of the name. Have you seen any Christian parents call their child *Jezebel*, after the ninth Century BC Phoenician pagan princess and queen of Israel. Jezebel was depicted in the Old Testament's Books of Kings as the most dangerous seductress and the wickedest of women, denounced as a murderer, prostitute and enemy of God. Whilst in recent years, many scholars and feminists have put forward a more balanced assessment of *Jezebel's* troubled reign, her reputation remains as originally set in the minds of most Christians, filtering through to the wider world. Today, the name, Jezebel is associated with evil and female depravity - it was adopted for World War II missiles. Another biblical name that is unlikely to be given to a Christian child is *Judas* after Judas Iscariot; one of Jesus Christ's twelve disciplines, who betrayed him. The name Judas, which used to mean praise, has come to mean traitor, associated with male treachery and betrayal. Today, the name Judas is often used to accuse someone of betrayal. If you are running for presidency, would you want to run with the name *Judas*? Not to mention *Adolf* or *Hitler*. Because of the stigma with the Nazi dictator, Adolf Hitler, these names are almost never given to any newborn and they have virtually disappeared from use.

On a much lighter note, there is a theatrical superstition around the usage of the name Macbeth from the Shakespeare play, in the theatre. Unless an actor is performing in Macbeth on stage, he will avoid the use of the name. Actors substitute the word 'Macbeth' with *The Scottish Play,* if they need to refer to the play in the theatre. If an actor says, 'Macbeth' in the theatre, he or she will be asked to step outside the theatre building, spin around three times, spit three times, curse and then knock on the door to be allowed back in. This may be why I have yet to meet a theatre actor called Macbeth.

So, where possible, your name should reflect who you are and be target-oriented. Ultimately, a great name will not do the job of your personal brand on its own. It is what you do with the name that counts.

Life is not a matter of creating a special name for ourselves, but of uncovering the name we have always had.

RICHARD ROHR

Priest, author and inspirational speaker

"I'm not changing my name. Remember that I have won a certain reputation with it, and I don't feel like beginning over again with a fresh name. Besides, my real name sounds even crazier. I was christened Georgette Lizette!"

GOOGIE WITHERS
Actress

EXERCISE 13

- Imagine your name inside the heads and hearts and on the tongues of your target audience.
  - Does it engage them at an emotional level?
  - Is it distinctive, sensory and memorable?
  - Does it reflect your character, personality and personal brand?
- What do you want your target audience to think when your name is mentioned?
- Can your name be pronounced easily?
- Does it have a back story?
- Is it fitting to the image you aspire to?

I wish my name was Brian because sometimes people would misspell my name and call me Brain. That's like a free compliment and you don't even gotta be smart to notice it.

MITCH HEDBERG
Comedian

"The happiest, most fulfilled people I know aren't those with the most material things. They are the people who know that their lives have value in the world around them."

STEDMAN GRAHAM

9.2. YOUR PERSONAL STORY

When you stand and share your story in an empowering way, your story will heal you and your story will heal somebody else.

IYANIA VANZANT
Inspirational speaker and author

There is real value in telling the story that propelled you to this journey, to your purpose and greater future. Every great personal brand has a compelling story behind it. It is often a story of what is possible not probable, of perseverance and hope. It highlights any similarities between your life and the lives of your target audience. It is through your story that you capture, inspire and engage your audience. And your audience will be happy to hear it repeatedly because they want to understand how you leveraged the cards you were dealt. The greater news is that if they like your story, they will share it with their target audience, who will share it with their audience.

Your personal story will help all your possible audiences to understand your brand statements, values, purpose, and why they connect or can connect with you. So it is an important tool for sharing your personal brand message and for creating intimacy between you and your audience. If you don't have a story that connects with and has an impact on your target audience, they will not understand or care about your brand message.

"Logos and branding are so important. In a big part of the world, people cannot read French or English ... but are great at remembering signs."

KARL LAGERFELD
Fashion designer and photographer

EXERCISE 14

Please write down your answers to the following questions:

- What is the key story that defines who you are today?
- How does your story connect with the lives and aspirations of your target audience?

9.3. YOUR VISUAL IDENTITY

A picture is worth a thousand words.

NAPOLEON BONAPARTE,
General and emperor

Your visual identity is your personal brand made visual. It is a vivid visual symbol or image; *your personal logo*, and the associated design elements that make your brand visually distinctive, generate recognition for you and announce you to the world. In creating your symbol, remember that it is not just what you communicate that matters, but what people hear. A vivid representation of your brand in its logo and packaging should convey the meaning of your brand visually and clearly, and help people to remember you. Your visual story wields special power because it remains in people's mind long after they've forgotten your words. Just like a picture, a symbol can speak a thousand words - louder, faster, more clearly and creating a lasting memory.

EXERCISE 15

Design your future. Start with a logo.

JAROD KINTZ
Writer

Imagine that you are going to sell yourself without words. What image would you use? Draw a rough draft of this image. This image is the first draft of your personal logo - a visual representation of everything you stand for. Make sure you've chosen a symbol that is vivid, a good representation of everything you stand for, challenging you to continue growing and operating within your values. Your symbol needs to be able to stand on its own. If you have to explain it, then it is not communicating your brand's message.

9.4. YOUR PERSONAL AND BUSINESS PRESENTATION

Know first, who you are; and then adorn yourself accordingly.

EPICTETUS
Philosopher

Your personal and business presentation is of tremendous importance in projecting the feeling and message of your personal brand. The way you dress, the way your home looks and the way your business - your office or studio, website, blog, and so on - looks is the best brand-building tool of all. So make yourself, your home and your website as attractive, well presented, accessible and brand-obsessive as possible. If your lifestyle involves regular contact with the public, you may benefit from the advice of a good stylist, who can help you to build an effective wardrobe featuring some unique elements that reflects your brand word, statements and mantra. An effective wardrobe will flatter you and tell the story of your brand vividly.

If your target audience includes first class clients and customers, you will need a first class office or studio. You may also need the services of an interior decorator, a web designer, a graphic designer, photographer, or other specialist to help you design the visible elements of your life and business. Your goal is to make sure that both your personal and business packaging illustrates and illuminates the message and promise of your personal brand instantly and consistently. Avoid any visual contradictions. A consistent identity is crucial for establishing your brand.

In Washington… the appearance of power is therefore almost as important as the reality of it. In fact, the appearance is frequently its essential reality.

HENRY KISSINGER

Fifty-sixth United States Secretary of State, 1973-77, and Nobel Prize winner

"Make sure everyone in your boat is rowing, not drilling holes... Know your circle."

UNKNOWN

9.4.1. YOUR INNER CIRCLE

Surround yourself only with people who are going to lift you higher.

OPRAH WINFREY

Your inner circle includes your spouse, boyfriend or girlfriend, parents, siblings and close friends, that you spend non-business hours with. They play an important role in your social and business world and they can be your strongest personal brand asset or liability. The way they present themselves also communicates *who you are* to your target audience and influence your audience's perception of you. If your spouse, relatives and friends are charming, dress and behave like ladies and gentlemen, and confirm that you are *who you say you are*, it will convince your audience of your integrity and strengthen your personal brand. Conversely, if they are offensive or politically incorrect - racist, sexist, with dirty and offensive jokes and views - they undermine or sabotage your personal brand in front of your audience, who might assume that their views are also yours. Depending on your audience and their religion and politics, your inner circle's controversial and offensive views can get you into trouble, costing you your reputation.

You need to be aware of the effect your inner circle's behaviour have on your personal brand. If they are a liability to your personal brand, then you have to take steps to limit any damage they may cause you and, if needs must, distance yourself from them. You may insist on going out solo, keeping them in the closet, or tactfully, tenderly and respectfully, explain that there are certain standards of behaviour that you require from those that share your life. These are non-negotiable.

"Nothing succeeds like the appearance of success."

CHRISTOPHER LASCH
Historian and Social Critic

EXERCISE 16

Please consider each of the following questions and write down your answers.

- What is your personal presentation saying at the moment? Does it communicate your brand message that you've taken pains to craft, or is it sabotaging the message of your brand?

- Does your personal style reflect your brand?

- Does your inner circle enhance or undermine your personal brand?

- What does your home, office or studio say about you and your work? Do the walls of your office or studio communicate the special story of who you are, your interests and your achievements? Design elements such as a beautiful painting or a stunning landscape photograph can serve as an initial point of interest and conversation with your clients.

- What does your business card say about you? What impression does it make? Does it communicate your point of difference? Does it have an attractive design and your logo? Is it memorable and distinctive?

- What story does your website and blog tell? Is your website and blog smart, quick and clear? Do you need a custom website and blog to tell your story better?

- What adjustments, changes or improvements do you need to make to reflect your personal brand in your personal and business presentation?

Don't let me be misunderstood.

MONALISA

CHAPTER

10. STEP III: DISTRIBUTE YOUR PERSONAL BRAND

That's it baby, when you got it, flaunt it! Flaunt it!

MEL BROOKS

Zero Mostel, *The Producers*, 1968

No matter how compelling your personal brand is and how great and wonderful its message and promise, you still need to introduce it and get visibility for it by communicating everything you've created in a clear and effective way. The best way to do this is through personal publicity. Personal publicity is an intimate and the most effective way of introducing and selling yourself to a broad audience in a positive and compelling way. It provides you with the tools and channels for sharing your personal brand, its message and the value it provides.

So at Step III, you will need to develop and implement a dynamic and comprehensive personal publicity plan that will help you to share the story and message of your personal brand, anywhere and everywhere that you interact with your target audience. Begin by charting out every way that you interact with your audience and the wider world, making sure that the story, message and promise of your brand - *who you are, what you do, your vision, your purpose, the value you provide* - are communicated clearly in a memorable, harmonious and consistent manner.

"If you wish in this world to advance,
Your merits you're bound to enhance;
You must stir and stump it,
and blow your own trumpet.
Or, trust me, you haven't a chance."

SIR WILLIAM SCHWENCK GILBERT
Dramatist, librettist and illustrator

So how do you communicate Brand You?

Personal publicity means bringing yourself to the attention of others. Personal publicity develops and sharpens your image, draws attention to your activities and achievements, and invites opportunities for advancement by making people aware of you.

ANNE MARIE RICCITELLI

Press representative for the American Broadcasting Co

There is literally no limit to the ways you can go about sharing the story and message of your personal brand. The hardest part is getting started.

- ***Start with the people around you***: distributing your personal brand begins with the person sitting next to you on the train, at your hairdresser's, at church or your club. Tell them and show them what it is like to be around you. Leave millions of impressions of your brand everywhere you go.

- ***Word-of-mouth reviews***: find ways to nurture every part of your target audience. What your friends, customers, clients, and business associates say about you and the value you and your brand provide is your most important distribution vehicle. Word of mouth on you is very powerful.

- ***Attend events***: people get to know you and your brand from what you tell them and from a third party. So get out there and share your personal brand and experience other personal brands.

- ***Speak at events***: this is a great way to promote your brand and its assets. People automatically assume you are an expert on whatever topic you speak. This attracts the attention of those who are interested in the promise of your brand.

- ***Create your own events***: this is an even greater way to share your vision with others, show case your abilities and assert your value. People will start seeing you as the go to authority for your key brand assets.

- ***Write a great book***: The printed word is very powerful. Nothing gives you greater credibility, an expert status and maximum exposure as a book, which clearly articulates your key ideas and your collection of wisdom on your passion, or your key successes and failures for your target audience. They say that the author is the expert and many members of your target audience will see your book as evidence that you are the expert, if they glean valuable information on your subject matter from it. This could even create a paradigm shift for them, if your book successfully addresses some of the issues they are facing. This will lead to great word-of-mouth on you. A great book will also create a buzz about your personal brand, giving it national exposure, generating extra income for you and opening doors to many more opportunities, such as collaborations with people who are interested in what you are doing, partnerships, and similar.

The list of potential distribution channels is endless. The important thing to remember is that every channel you choose matters. Success is very much dependent on how well you blend:

- ***the substance of your brand*** - your story, message and promise; with
- ***the style of your brand*** - your personal brand packaging;

and your commitment to engaging all your target audience in a clear, memorable and powerful way. Keep asking yourself the following:

Is my message and packaging distinctive, compelling and engaging enough to stand out and be noticed in a crowded world?

You must become a great communicator to convey your personal brand effectively to all your possible audiences. If this is a skill you lack, the good news is that it can be mastered. You may need to engage the services of a communications expert to help you develop and implement a dynamic and comprehensive personal publicity plan.

The world's a stage, and I want the brightest spot.

DAVID LEE ROTH

Rock vocalist, actor and author

"Of course, I'm a publicity hound. Aren't all crusaders? How can you accomplish anything unless people know what you are trying to do?"

VIVIEN KELLEMS
Inventor, public speaker and politician

EXERCISE 17

PR brings endorsement and credibility to the message.

MICHAEL MENDENHALL

Chief marketing and communications officer, Fusion-io

Check your home, wardrobe, office or studio, website, blog, Facebook, Twitter and Linked-in pages, YouTube channel, business documents, keynote speeches, after dinner speeches and social invitations to answer the following questions:

- Are they telling your personal brand story?
- Do your word and statements feature?
- Do you have quality content, clearly articulating your key ideas, your collection of wisdom on your passion and your key successes for your target audience?

CHAPTER

11. STEP IV: LIVE YOUR PERSONAL BRAND, LIVE UP TO YOUR DREAMS

A brand is a living entity – and it is enriched or undermined cumulatively over time ... the product of a thousand small gestures.

MICHAEL DAMMANN EISNER

Businessman and CEO of Walt Disney, 1984-2005

So you have defined and developed your personal brand word, statements and packaging. And you've looked at every way that you interact with your target audience and the wider world, and made sure that the story, message and promise of your brand is communicated clearly, in a harmonious and consistent manner. However, whilst all the above will score some points with your target audience and how they perceive you, it is only when you can match these perceptions with daily actions and behaviour that your personal brand will really become real to them. As the poet John Keats said, *"Nothing ever becomes real till it is experienced"*. It is only when your target audience experiences your personal brand through your actions that they will see the integrity of your message. Henry Ford, founder of the Ford Motor Company, said that, *"You can't build a reputation on what you are going to do"*. Action always speaks louder than words.

"It takes 20 years to build a reputation and five minutes to ruin it. If you think about that, you'll do things differently."

WARREN BUFFET
Business magnate and philanthropist

The fourth stage of the personal branding process is about *living your brand - bringing Brand You to life.* This is the most challenging stage as it requires you to stay focused on the message and promise of your brand 24/7/365. This is a big responsibility. Your job at this stage is to make sure that everything you do is not only congruent and consistent with the promise of your personal brand but also adds to its value.

When creating a personal brand, almost every protagonist is positive and believes in the positive message and promise of his or her brand. The crux of all our hard work is that we will maintain and reflect this positivity in our behaviour and actions throughout the life of our personal brand. But sometimes, we don't act like the person we want the world to see. The human condition is that sometimes we have personal stresses, down moods or even up moods that lead us to actions or behaviour that may undermine our personal brand. But having the responsibility of living our brand, 24/7/365, means that we cannot, ever, let any mood undermine the integrity of our personal brand. There is no room for emotional unpredictability.

The tough truth about having a personal brand is that nobody really cares that you are having an off day or that you are only human. Whilst some of your target audience, especially your loved ones, may understand that you are having an off day and that you are who you say you are, outside your intimate circle, you are simply *who you appear to be.* Even if your loved ones forgive you many off days, they will not be able to keep the picture of your brand you want them to have in their hearts and minds after any off day. Your personal brand is always on record. Your brand takes no holiday. To maintain its attributes and message, it has to be the same every time it is exposed to others. Every off day changes how all your target audience feel and think about your brand, irrespective of their continuing love for you.

"Branding requires commitment; commitment to continual reinvention; striking chords with people to stir their emotions; and commitment to imagination. It is easy to be cynical about such things, much harder to be successful."

SIR RICHARD BRANSON
Business magnate and CEO of Virgin

Personal brands are more about feelings rather than rational thought. Years of positive brand behaviour can be undermined by one negative act.

So by hook or by crook, to keep our brand, we must deliver the positive outcomes it promised at its creation consistently. It is only when we discipline ourselves to act and deliver our brand's promise consistently that we confirm to our target audience that we are who and what we say we are. Your brand message and value is communicated and reinforced one action at a time. In playwriting and screenwriting, when introducing or presenting a character, a good writer adopts a very useful phrase in his or her work, *show - don't tell.* This phrase also works for personal branding because it inspires authenticity, which is the most important element in living your personal brand. You have to show rather than tell who you are or what you do. Rather than saying what you are or what you do, *simply be or do.*

Ultimately, your behaviour and actions are your personal brand. They either enhance or undermine it. So, you need to make sure that everything you do is congruent with your brand and keep building value in it by consistently adding value to the lives of others. Living your personal brand means living each day doing what is required not what is easy - and going to bed each night knowing that you've made a difference to somebody's life.

You also need to keep stretching your brand assets. *Staying still is the kiss of death for any brand.* You've got to keep your brand in constant motion; take an action that reinforces and stretches it every day, step up to higher levels of the old things in your brand and seek new opportunities and projects that deliver or exceed its promise. If you keep stretching your brand, you will continue to grow as a person.

"Whatever your life's work is, do it well. A man should do his job so well that the living, the dead, and the unborn could do it no better."

DR. MARTIN LUTHER KING, JR.

EXERCISE 18

Create a *Living your Brand* plan. This is a list of the key actions or activities that you will undertake daily, weekly, monthly to:

- build, enhance and distribute your personal brand; and
- deliver value to you and your target audience - *those you serve.*

Each activity will have a list of the principal things you need to do to get that activity completed. Keep asking yourself the following questions:

- What is my brand saying at the moment? What is required to make it stronger, to keep it relevant and valuable? Brands that grow and endure are relevant. To be relevant, simply continue to provide concrete and outstanding value to others.
- What are the long term implications of the choices I am making today? Am I enriching or undermining my personal brand?
- Am I delivering the promise of my brand? What can I do to build greater value for my target audience? Don't ever take your target audience for granted. Take every opportunity to invest in it. Keep in touch with any changes in its needs and make thoughtful adjustments when necessary.

"Do you want to know who you are? Don't ask. Act! Action will delineate and define you."

THOMAS JEFFERSON
President of the United States: 1801 to 1809

Personal brands require a body and soul commitment to thrive. Personal brands that stand out and endure are those who offer the greatest value, keep their promise and build upon it. Successfully establishing your personal brand - *your reputation* - depends much on your effort and passion. At the end of the day, people do not really care about *who you are*. What people care about is *how good you are at who you are.*

AFTERTHOUGHTS

There is no finish line. ...
Beating the competition is relatively easy;
But beating yourself is a never-ending commitment.

NIKE 1977 AD CAMPAIGN

As with Nike's 1977 ad campaign, personal branding is a lifelong project that involves a series of challenges and opportunities that never end. Maintaining, enhancing and keeping your brand relevant is a lifelong adventure and competition with yourself that requires you to constantly:

- reach beyond the limitations of your mind for your next biggest possibility and to grow into it;
- bring the extraordinary into your life.

Never stop aspiring to play a bigger game, to make a greater difference and to exceed what you've already accomplished until your life stops.

Congratulations! You've made it to the end. I hope you now have a better idea of *who you are* and where you are going. Understanding *who you are* and *where you are going* will give you more control of your life. And you'd be much further along in building a powerful personal brand.

"Decide what you want to be – pay the price and be what you want to be."

JOHN A. WIDTSOE
Author, scientist and academic

The main benefit of building your personal brand is the joy of awakening each morning to a life you've designed, and to have the chance to serve somebody and to really matter. There may be days when you're likely to experience some discomfort, fatigue, even darkness. At such moments, it may help to remember that history has shown that the most successful lives were filled with many moments of darkness. Every dark moment presents us with two choices: to stop the journey or to keep going. The only thing that happens if we stop is *regret*. To keep going is much harder, but always the right choice. The single trait of all successful people is their resilience through dark periods; they never stop. They endure. They understand that life is incredibly challenging. They understand that none of us gets out of here alive and that, in the end, what really matters is the difference we made and the legacy we left - something that will inspire others long after we've gone. Like them, you will come to see that the road to something great is mostly paved by pain, discomfort and despair. You will learn that despair makes one strong and that its accompanying darkness often brings character, polish and direction. So,

Don't bail; the best gold is at the bottom of barrels of crap.

PROFESSOR RANDY PAUSCH

Professor of Computer Science

Some of the greatest works in history were created during incredibly challenging periods in the lives of their creators.

- Consider Martin Luther King Jr's famous gospel of freedom '***Letter from Birmingham City Jail***', written in a cramped cell in Birmingham, Alabama on 13 April, 1963, after being arrested in downtown Birmingham on a Good Friday. This letter showed Martin's fundamental belief that all those who are oppressed will eventually demand their birthright of freedom. It became a leading document of the civil rights movement, remaining one of the best human rights arguments in history. His invigorating letter demonstrates how he responded to his immediate circumstances that Easter weekend - resolutely and with no sign at all of giving up on his vision for the future of blacks in America. His words in this letter continue to inspire many human rights activists and still resonate in many hearts 52 years later.

Injustice anywhere is a threat to justice everywhere. We are caught in an inescapable network of mutuality, tied in a single garment of destiny. Whatever affects one directly, affects all indirectly.

DR. MARTIN LUTHER KING, JR.

- Ludwig van Beethoven's most beautiful and extraordinary body of music, which stands at the outer limits of human accomplishment, was composed in the last ten years of his life, when he had lost his hearing. According to Harvey Sachs, author of *The Ninth: Beethoven and the World in 1824*, Beethoven wanted his music during this period, "Not only to be enjoyed, but to help humanity to emerge from the darkness into the light". His final symphony - Symphony No. 9 in D minor, Op. 125, also known as *the Choral*, which he completed in 1824, is his most towering achievement and is considered by some as one of the greatest and most influential classical music pieces ever written.

O you men who think or say that I am malevolent, stubborn or misanthropic, how greatly do you wrong me. You do not know the secret cause which makes me seem that way to you and I would have ended my life - it was only my art that held me back. Ah, it seemed impossible to leave the world until I had brought forth all that I felt was within me.

LUDWIG VAN BEETHOVEN,
The Heiligenstadt Testament, 6 October, 1802

"There is only one success: To be able to spend your life in your own way."

CHRISTOPHER MORLEY
Journalist, novelist and poet

- John Milton wrote his epic poem, *Paradise Lost*, in 1667 while blind and at a time before braille, recorded books or any of the modern technologies that assist visually impaired people today. Though blindness was like an intellectual death sentence in his time, he endured its limitations and his numerous personal difficulties and was determined not to allow it to stop his artistic dreams, particularly his poetry and prose, which reflect his passion for freedom and self determination.

In my blindness, I enjoy in no inconsiderable degree the favour of the Deity, who regards me with more tenderness and compassion in proportion, as I am able to behold nothing but himself.

JOHN MILTON
Poet and polemicist

And there are many more examples of outstanding achievements during periods of adversity. The greatest miracle of all, human birth itself, even with outstanding modern medical developments for managing pain, still involves a degree of pain. If humanity avoided pain, none of us would be here today. Human birth is one pain that we are grateful and thankful for.

I hope that you will also come to see that living your life vitally, on your own terms and for something greater than your own success, is the greatest privilege you can hope for. Your greatest asset is you - yourself. Nurture it. Whatever it takes, become your best self. Don't you dare take the easy road. Be all that you can be. You have what it takes. And you've come a long way since the beginning of this book. I believe that there are greater things to come. For the rest of your journey, from this moment on, I want you to wake up each morning voicing these three phrases:

my life, my choice, my legacy

I hope that these phrases will hold you accountable for your choices for each day. I promise you that, with time, you will come to see how well a powerful personal brand will have served you in achieving your life's purpose. In the evening of your life, I want you to look back at the extraordinary success story that is You.

Life can only be understood backwards, but it must be lived forwards.

SØREN KIERKEGAARD
Philosopher, theologian and author

Let me finish with my first questions to you. This time, I want you to write down your answers.

- What is your personal brand currently saying about you?
  - Is it clear and positive?
  - What does it promise?
  - What value does it represent?
  - Is it working effectively for your vision?
- *Is it the distinctive, compelling and enduring brand you need for your greater future?*
- *Do you need to develop or expand it?* Standing water goes stagnant.

Dear heart, we embrace the song and the story and all our gifts because the world has such great need, and because the world exceedingly rejoices, and because there is no sadder thing than to leave this world having never really shown up.

CARRIE NEWCOMER
A Permeable Life: Poems & Essays

Embrace your potential.
Live forever through your legacy!

MONALISA

Thank you for spending this time with me. It has been a pleasure, privilege and honour to have the opportunity to share my observations, insights and experiences with you.

I pray that this book will give you the confidence, ability and power to become extraordinary, recognised and valued in you world.

Be a story worth telling,

XO,

MonaLisa

MONALISA

MONALISA

POSTSCRIPT

If you'd like to arrange a personal consultation with me or would like me to speak at your club, company or association about *Personal Branding, Building an Extraordinary Profile* or *Personal Packaging*, please contact me at:

monalisa@monalisainternational.com

Seminars and Workshops

I host seminars and workshops throughout the year in the UK, Europe and Africa on *Building an Extraordinary Profile, Personal Branding* and *Personal Packaging*. Readers of this book are invited to enrol at a special discounted price. I also hold private personal branding and image consultations and counselling. I invite you to email me at the address above or call me at:

+44-(0)20 8599 1832 to learn more about the seminars, workshops or for an individual consultation.

Please also let me know if this book was helpful to you and share your successes, questions and comments with me.

Thank you,

MonaLisa

MONALISA

www.monalisainternational.com
www.monalisalifestyle.com
twitter.com/MonaLisa_I

MONALISA

ABOUT THE AUTHOR

MONALISA
INTERNATIONAL

WWW.MONALISAINTERNATIONAL.COM

MonaLisa Chukwuma, founder and president of MonaLisa International (www.monalisainterantional.com), a fine art photography and image Consultancy and creator of the MONALISA brand, is an image maker and author of image building and management texts including, ***Building An Extraordinary Profile***, ***Personal Packaging***, ***Fashion's Classic Twelve*** and ***Daily Image Mantras.***

MonaLisa's Image Consultancy transforms individuals, consultants, executives, entrepreneurs and politicians into strong, compelling and enduring brands. MonaLisa advises her clients on personal and business packaging and on how to increase their visibility and online footprint through personal publicity, so that they attract all their potential audiences and achieve personal and professional goals that propel them to the top of their field and help them to build an extraordinary profile.

MonaLisa runs seminars and workshops and shoots photography projects in the UK, Europe and Africa. She is an advocate of women's and human rights. MonaLisa believes in taking chances, in building her own path in life and in living her passion. When she's not writing, you can easily find her cooking, horse riding, reading an old book, watching movies, exploring London or blogging her own daily adventures. She is addicted to learning about herself, about others and about life. MonaLisa lives in London, United Kingdom.

MONALISA

ACKNOWLEDGEMENTS

My grand appreciation for this book goes to:

- The brilliant Chris Day and the entire team at Filament Publishing - the publishers of this book. Chris has been lovely from the first day, I spoke with him on the phone. He was a brilliant force, who saw the potential in this book and supported it all the way. His vision, intelligent guidance and encouragement helped me through every step. Chris has been great to work with and made this process enjoyable.

- My incredible editor Palden Jenkins, who casted his 20/20 eyes over all my words and worked faithfully with me to complete this book. Palden is one of the most articulate, meticulous and positive people I've worked with. His wisdom, sharp and insightful editing skills were impressive and inspired me.

- The creative genius that is Melissa Love, who designed my book cover in her usual simple and elegant style. Melissa is without any doubt one the most talented graphic artists in the UK.

- All my amazing clients and workshop participants who have inspired me. I am so proud of each and every one of them for harnessing the power of their compelling personal brands.

- Finally, I want to thank my family, the great loves of my life. Thank you for everything.

A thousand thanks,

MonaLisa

MONALISA

CHAPTER SUMMARIES

CHAPTER 1 SUMMARY

- We all have a personal brand. From the Prime Minister David Cameron, to the artist Sam Smith, to your grandfather, we all have one.
- Your personal brand is your reputation. It is what people think, know, feel and say about you when you're not in front of them.
- Your personal brand communicates who you are, what is unique about you, what you do, what you uniquely bring to the table and its benefits to others.
- Every action you take and some actions that you don't take shapes it.
- It is important to understand how you are currently perceived by others and whether this perception is working for or against you.

CHAPTER 2 SUMMARY

- Your life will become more meaningful, powerful and valuable when guided by your personal brand.
- Building a powerful personal brand will separate and place you well above your competition, helping you to leverage your points of distinction and to develop a thriving professional career or business.
- Your personal brand will help you to manage your name and others' perception of you, especially in the business world where perception is everything.
- A high quality personal brand gives you a compelling identity that is easily and instantly recognised in our overcrowded market place.
- Your brand shows the unique value you provide, that you're credible and that others can therefore pay a higher price for your worth.
- It enhances your self-knowledge and gives you authenticity. When you truly understand who you are and where you want to go, and when you commit to this, your life becomes more meaningful and fulfilling.
- Personal branding offers resilience and security, because it will remain fundamentally the same, no matter how the economy or your life evolves.
- Your brand provides you with a system for defining your purpose and life goals. It helps you to use your talents and abilities to achieve these goals more quickly and effectively.
- Most importantly, personal branding will dramatically increase your influence, enabling you to make a bigger difference.

CHAPTER 3 SUMMARY

- To create a distinctive, compelling and enduring personal brand that will attract and engage all your possible audiences, you need to be rid of any inhibitors or blocks that undermine your self-image, stopping you from honest and bold self-expression.

- How you feel and what you think of yourself matters because it affects your behaviour. Your behaviour controls your future.

- You must get past your self-doubt and stop the negative and crazy chatter in your head that tells you that you are not good enough, so that you can embrace your potential and achieve your destiny.

- You don't have to be the best to create outstanding value. To be extraordinary, you need to focus on the unique way that you enrich the lives of others.

- Anyone who is growing and making a difference is struggling and stretching. It's not as effortless as it may seem. Nothing worthwhile is really ever achieved without a struggle.

- Any time you try to adapt yourself to what you think will please others, you weaken your personal brand.

- Your brand cannot and should not appeal to everyone.

- You honour yourself when you vigorously advocate what you believe, align your actions with who you are and go after what you want.

- Surround yourself only with people who believe in you, lift you up and make you stronger.

- The time for growth will never be absolutely right, so don't set it aside until another day. Growth starts with a decision. One step at a time, with each step improving the landscape under which you are growing.

- We have so much to learn from the actions and sacrifices of the great men and women in our time, who faced their enemies, risking their lives on the possibility that they could make the world a better place for all.

- We too must confront what or who frightens us and get involved in making our world a better place to live.

CHAPTER 4 SUMMARY

- You have a unique set of talents, abilities and potentials that nobody else has. Because of this, nobody's path in life is the same as yours.

- You must never fundamentally change what makes you unique - your talents, skills, values and the way you see the world. Who you are is where your power lies, where your magic lies.

- Recognising your unique qualities and devoting your life to developing them to their full potential will help you to operate at your very best.

- For talent to yield high performance and enduring success, it must be accompanied by focused, excruciating, long-term hard work.

- It takes years and years of practice and commitment to become great at anything you do that involves a skill or expertise.

CHAPTER 5 SUMMARY

The seven main components to your personal brand are:

- Your one word - the single word that sums up all that you aim for in life.

- Your who you are and what you do statements - who you are at your core and the value you add to the lives of your target audience.

- Your target audience - who you serve and who you want to serve in the future.

- Your purpose and vision - the fixed purpose around which everything you do in your life revolves, and who you want to become or what you want to achieve in your life.

- Your core values - the values that guide your decisions and behaviour.

- Your brand mantra - a short, inspiring and motivating phrase or sentence that captures the spirit, uniqueness and raison d'être of your personal brand. This sentence sets your personal brand boundaries, stopping you from over-reaching them. This is for your own use.

- Your tagline - an inspiring and memorable phrase or sentence that captures the essence of your personal brand's promise to your target audience. This is for use in your outreach.

CHAPTER 6 SUMMARY

To stand out, your personal brand:

- should communicate a clear and simple message.
- must say something different and be as distinctive as your fingerprint.
- must be meaningful to you and your target audience.
- should be so positive and compelling that it inspires and invigorates others and invites opportunities.
- should provide real and lasting value to others.
- must be authentic. Who you are and what you say must be integrated with what you do.
- packaging must convey its meaning visually and clearly.

CHAPTER 7 SUMMARY

- The best way to create an outstanding brand is to provide an outstanding value in everything you do.

- Every powerful brand is characterised by a logically constructed set of brand-building steps.

- The key personal brand-building steps are:

  - Define and develop your personal brand,

  - Package your personal brand,

  - Distribute your personal brand, and

  - Live your personal brand.

CHAPTER 8 SUMMARY

- The first step to building your personal brand is to clearly articulate who you are.
- Here, you want to develop a narrative that clearly shows what is unique about you - your values, insights, aspirations, skills and abilities, experiences - and how your skills and experiences can add value in a given context.
- You want to get really clear internally about what you do, why you do it, what you do not want to do, where you want to be, who you serve, what you bring to the table and its benefits to others.
- You want to help others to understand and visualise what it is like to be around you, the value you add to others' lives and what you will be remembered for.
- You will be remembered not for your achievements but for how you've impacted the lives of others.

CHAPTER 9 SUMMARY

- The second step to building your personal brand is packaging.
- Here, you will be creating a distinctive and attractive look for your personal brand. Your brand packaging will ensure:
    - your name and how it is perceived by your target audience;
    - your personal story - the key story or stories that define who you are today;
    - your visual identity - your logo and the other design elements that generate recognition for you; and
    - your personal and business presentation tells the story of your personal brand perfectly.
- You should also be aware of the effect your inner circle's behaviour has on your personal brand. If they are a liability to your brand, you must take steps to limit any damage they may cause you or distance yourself from them.

CHAPTER 10 SUMMARY

- No matter how compelling your personal brand is, you still need to introduce it to your target audience, in a clear and memorable way.

- The best way to do this is through personal publicity. Personal publicity is the most effective way of introducing and selling yourself to a broad audience.

- Start by charting out every way that you interact with your audience, making sure that the story, message and promise of your brand are communicated clearly in a harmonious and consistent manner.

- There are several ways that you can share the story and message of your personal brand - from word-of-mouth reviews and speaking at events to writing a great book.

- Success depends much on how well you blend *the substance of your brand* - your story, message and promise - with *the style of your brand* - your personal brand packaging.

CHAPTER 11 SUMMARY

- The fourth and final step of the personal branding process is about living your brand - manifesting the promise of your brand.
- This stage requires you to stay focused on the message and promise of your brand 24/7/365.
- You need to show that holy trinity of personal branding in all your actions - clarity, consistency and authenticity.
- Your brand is not what you say. Your brand is what people extrapolate from your daily actions.
- It is only when your audience experiences your personal brand through your actions that they will see the integrity of your message - that you are who you say you are.
- Ultimately, your behaviour and actions are your personal brand. They either enhance or undermine it.